To Harriette & Eddie,

Enjoy "your" journey!

all the best,

Dwayne
Ball

JOURNEY
WITH JULIAN

JOURNEY WITH JULIAN

DWAYNE BALLEN

SBI

STREBOR BOOKS

NEW YORK LONDON TORONTO SYDNEY

Strebor Books
P.O. Box 6505
Largo, MD 20792
http://www.streborbooks.com

This book is a work of nonfiction.

ISBN 978-1-59309-423-2
ISBN 978-1-4516-5953-5 (ebook)
LCCN 2011938321

First Strebor Books trade paperback edition April 2013

Cover design: www.mariondesigns.com
Cover photograph: © Keith Saunders/Marion Designs

10 9 8 7 6 5 4 3 2 1

Manufactured in the United States of America

For information regarding special discounts for bulk purchases,
please contact Simon & Schuster Special Sales at 1-866-506-1949
or business@simonandschuster.com

The Simon & Schuster Speakers Bureau can bring authors to your live event.
For more information or to book an event, contact the Simon & Schuster Speakers
Bureau at 1-866-248-3049 or visit our website at www.simonspeakers.com.

To Julian, without you there would be no journey.

WHAT IS AUTISM?

Autism Spectrum Disorders (ASD) are a range of complex neurodevelopment disorders, characterized by social impairments, communication difficulties, and restricted, repetitive, and stereotyped patterns of behavior. Although ASD varies significantly in character and severity, it occurs in all ethnic and socioeconomic groups and affects every age group. Experts estimate that one out of eighty-eight children age eight will have an ASD.

—From the National Institutes of Health's National Institute of Neurological Disorders and Stroke

FOREWORD
BY BRANFORD MARSALIS

I remember the first time I met the Ballen family at a neighbor's Christmas party. I didn't notice Julian to be any different than the other kids at first. But, gradually, the lack of eye contact gave me a hint that he might have autism.

My brother, MBoya, was diagnosed with autism at the age of three. Since he was ten years younger, I didn't have a lot of interaction with MBoya until I was well into my twenties. Severely affected by autism, my brother cannot speak, and walks on his toes.

Julian, by comparison, is highly functioning. Nonetheless, I am more than aware of the ups and downs caring for a child with special needs.

Dwayne does a marvelous job of peeling away the curtain, so the reader can understand the everyday realities in his and Martina's lives. Julian is a special boy, blessed with special parents.

I hope you all enjoy the journey.

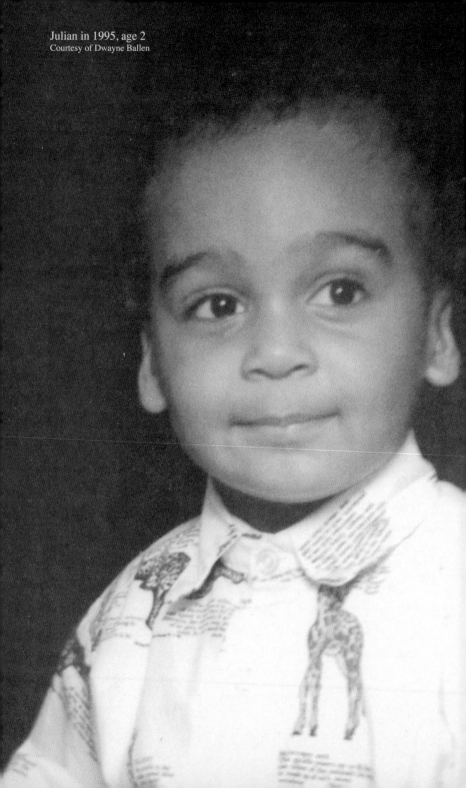

Julian in 1995, age 2
Courtesy of Dwayne Ballen

JULIAN

The first thing one usually notices is his smile: genuine, inviting and warming. Then it's his eyes—dancing with wonderment and innocence. As you gaze downward, awaiting your clasp, you are welcomed into his world by his outstretched arm and a handshake. "Hello. I'm Julian."

He is five feet nine inches tall, slender, but not skinny, in build. Most that greet him comment on how handsome he is. He has prompted not a few young ladies to turn their heads in double-takes upon seeing him. He has an affinity for Disney animated movies and animals. Though he is nearing his twentieth birthday, socially, there are aspects of his persona more in line with that of a ten-year-old.

He is my son and he has autism. Our family—my wife, Martina; Julian and his younger (by two years) brother, Jared—have been on this journey, through the world of autism, for nearly sixteen years. It's been unpredictable, enlightening and challenging. The highs have been soaring and the lows almost unbearable.

When we first received the diagnosis, we were not surprised. After prior conversations with friends who were doctors and several behavioral factors we had noticed, we knew, as Martina put it, "Something's up with our son." I would encourage all parents of young children who evince signs of unconventional development to be aggressive and dive in headfirst. If it is autism or another developmental disorder, it's better you know early and begin to address it rather than pretend it's simply a phase.

I will never forget the determination in Martina's voice. She was the one who first began to think about this, and spoke with my Uncle Harold when Julian was about two-and-a-half. "Uncle Harold, I think something might be different with Julian."

He replied, "Maybe it's a stage, terrible twos?"

She remained firm in her position. "No, something is not right."

And so began, though we didn't know it at the time, our entry into the world of autism.

Through it all, what has fortified us are unwavering love and support for Julian, the inspiration we draw from his resilience and strength, a fierce belief in his gifts and abilities and recognition that, despite the obstacles, there are other families in the autism community who face far greater hurdles. Experts place the number of individuals with autism who are mentally retarded to be anywhere from 70 to 85 percent. Julian is on the high-functioning end of the Autism Spectrum Disorders continuum, and for that, we are eternally thankful.

Though I was encouraged to pursue this book by a close friend, Rohena Miller, to whom I can never say thank you enough, for understanding, long before I did, that our story was one that should be shared with the world, I never would have followed through with it if Julian were not okay with the idea. I don't know that he will ever read this book, but I've had multiple conversations with him about the project. He will always know that it was born out of love and pride for him.

The book is a mixture of entries from the blog ("Journey With Julian") that is the foundation for the book and stories with deeper insight into our world. I hope it helps everyone dealing with autism to realize that the issues they face are shared by others. None of us should feel that we take this journey, into the world of autism, without support and understanding.

When Julian was diagnosed at age four, in 1997, one in 10,000 children were diagnosed with autism spectrum disorder. In 2012, the Centers for Disease Control and Prevention released updated—and staggering—numbers. It's now one in eighty-eight, with boys five times more likely than girls to have ASD. Given the numbers, it's understandable why those of us in the autism community feel a strong need to raise awareness within greater society. We must, as a larger community, prepare to integrate this "tsunami" of persons with autism into our world.

I asked Julian what he wanted people to get out of this book. At first he didn't really have a definite answer; this is not a topic he cares to spend much time discussing. However, I wouldn't let the conversation go, and after gentle pushing and challenging, on my part, he finally offered this: "I want them to know I'm happy with my Disney movies and animals and that I will have a great life."

There it was, all any parent could ever hope for—their child understanding who they were, finding comfort in that fact, and looking forward to a future of hope and optimism. It's moments like that in which my love, respect and admiration for my son swells. His is not a complicated view; he enjoys the subjects and items that comprise his specific "interest community" (most persons with autism have laser-like focus on certain interests), doesn't mind telling you about them, and derives unfiltered joy from being immersed in that particular world.

Julian has provided Martina and me with the full emotional experience as parents. For that we are forever indebted to our eldest son. He has made us feel "very" alive; no day with him is quite the same. As you read this book, I trust it will cause you to laugh, cry and to appreciate the world inhabited by the thousands of exceptional people like Julian.

Julian in 1998, age 5
Courtesy of Dwayne Ballen

WHY DOES HE FLAP HIS HANDS?

"What's that about?" my close friend Barry, who is blunt but always comes from a place of genuine concern, was asking about Julian's actions. He and I were sitting on the back deck of my house watching Julian, who was five at the time, run around in the yard. We were witnessing a definite routine. Julian, with his head down, would sprint for about five yards, stop, whirl around and retrace his path, all the while flapping his hands and emitting a sound that was a cross between a hum and a chant. He could do this nonstop for a half-hour before taking a short break, then resuming.

"It's what he does. Self-stimulation, it's part of his autism. This is a whole new world." Along with that answer, I gave Barry a look that suggested I wasn't quite sure, or maybe prepared for, what lay ahead. We were less than a year removed from his official diagnosis. Watching Julian occupy himself in this manner was something I'd become accustomed to. Though when I first saw this, I tried to curtail the activity.

I was standing on the balcony, upstairs in our house, which overlooked the den below. Our nanny, Gayle Stephens, was in the kitchen feeding Jared, and I was watching Julian pace back and forth, flap his hands and make that noise as though he had a motor running on low hum. This was only a few weeks prior to the meeting when doctors told us that Julian had autism. Watching him do this was slightly irritating to me; remember at this point, I was expecting traditional behavior. Plus, I was spending most of my time on the West Coast as an anchor for the Fox Sports Network. I wasn't around much and, therefore, I wasn't used to seeing this in Julian.

When he didn't immediately cease, upon my command, I walked downstairs, took ahold of his shoulders, smiled and firmly intoned, "Daddy said stop. Okay?" I searched his face for compliance. At the time, he would rarely look you directly in the eyes; this was no different. Convinced I had gotten my point across, I released him and watched as he went right back to his pacing, flapping and humming. This was autism; I just didn't know it yet.

What we came to learn, after the diagnosis, was that Julian was engaging in self-stimulation behavior, or stimming as it is colloquially known. Persons with autism engage in all forms of stimming for various reasons. Some utilize it to manage anxiety, fear, anger or negative emotions. It can be a release after a full day of conforming to the outside world. It can be a tool of self-regulation. It can be a coping mechanism. There are no definitive conclusions as to why people with autism self-stimulate. We just know they do it.

Fact is many of us stim. Do you know someone who constantly taps a pencil or pen? Bites their nails regularly? Martina has a habit of moving her legs in rapid motion while seated and watching television. I always ask her if she's going somewhere. In people with autism, the self-stimulation can appear extreme to us, neurotypicals. Usually the quality and quantity, of stim, is very different and considerable.

A teenager in one of Julian's summer camps walks rapidly, inside or outside. It helps him calm down. Some individuals rock back and forth; others use repetitive speech and phrasing. Whatever it is, it is almost always constant. When we better understood Julian's need to pace and flap his hands, we got him to the point that if he restricted his movement in certain situations that required more attentive posturing, say in church, then as soon as we got home, he could pace and flap until his heart was content.

Over the years, Julian's stimming has taken on different forms. First, there was the flapping and pacing. There was a period that produced a clicking noise from his throat, and then there was the need to go on daily walks alone in our neighborhood. He now has to touch objects as he walks by, or enters and exits a room. In addition to inanimate objects, he also has to touch Jared, Martina or me if we're in the room.

We have learned to roll with the flow when it comes to Julian and stimming. Just when we think we know what he'll do, it changes. However, there is one form of self-stimulation—at least I think it can be placed in that category—that has been a constant throughout his young life: drawing. He loves to draw and often, no matter the setting, will request a pen and paper. I've noticed when he appears uncomfortable in a situation, drawing helps him find a place of calm. For us, if it helps Julian get through the day and deal with the world, then it's good.

FEBRUARY 17, 2010 – MARCH 16, 2011

THIRTY-FIVE STEPS

FEBRUARY 17, 2010

I remember very well the day my son, Julian, came into the world. It was a late August morning filled with the brightness of sunshine, clear skies and the unlimited hopes and dreams my wife, Martina, and I harbored for our child. As I held this tiny wonder in my arms, I quickly began to envision his life as one heavily populated with achievements and awards the entire world would celebrate. For, you see, he was destined for greatness as we would give him every possible advantage. I imagined the conversation we would have when he had to decide between the Rhodes Scholarship and accepting lucrative offers to become a professional athlete. He would become a colossus, astride the worlds of business, civic life and philanthropy. This would be a man for the ages, one who would help make the world a better place. I actually imagined our trip to Oslo, Norway or Stockholm, Sweden for his Nobel Prize ceremony. Yes, I can get carried away. But such was the nature of our expectation for the life of our son.

Autism. The diagnosis was made when he was four years of age; Martina and I were at a loss, suddenly adrift in the uncertain waters of autism. Where would this new, unplanned journey take us? Were we prepared for the road ahead? Julian has turned out to be our chief navigator and instructor. From him we've learned so much about allowing someone to follow his or her own pathway. We also have, thanks to him, a much clearer sense of where the real values in life reside.

He first taught us patience and to be thankful for each singular moment of happiness. When he was three, he was not verbal. This (delayed speech) is very common in children with autism. His frustration at being unable to communicate through words led to constant and very loud tantrums. These outbursts sometimes led to his physical destruction of his room. He would knock over toys and rip artwork off the wall. It reached a point that we had to remove all items that were not firmly secured from his room. These fits were his only outlet of expression for the first few years of his life, and we, along with our incredibly patient nanny, Gayle, had to ride the storm out with Julian.

The image of Martina's tear-filled look of hopelessness, when she wondered if she would ever be able to have a conversation with Julian, is seared in my memory. "Will he ever be able to say, 'I love you, Mommy'?" was her plaintive query. Then one evening, after a particularly trying day with him, as she watched him play with toy animals in his room, he turned to her, looking directly at her, which was a rarity, and without any prompting said, "Mommy." This single-word utterance unleashed a torrent of emotion in her as she engulfed him in a joyful embrace that seemed to go on for hours.

This seemingly simple moment brought quite a bit of joy into our world. Julian had spoken. His verbal development would continue to be quite a challenge, but it did progress. To our delight he hasn't stopped talking and, today he is full of thoughts and opinions on his favorite topics: animals, Africa, Disney animated films and Egyptian mythology.

Thanks to Julian, I can share with you the meaning of courage. It's the thirty-five steps he takes from the vehicle to the front door of his high school every morning when I drop him off. As most of you know, sixteen-year-olds can be about as compassionate as Simon Cowell during the early rounds of *American Idol*. Everyone wants to be cool and fit in with the crowd. Well, Julian doesn't. His physical appearance reveals nothing of his autism; this can make it even more challenging for him sometimes. He's quite handsome, has his mom's looks, but he's very different from most of his peers. Socially, he can't connect with his fellow students. He doesn't have any friends at school and often eats lunch with a favorite teacher. He likes girls but is unable to engage them. Academics are very difficult for him. Think about when you were sixteen, tough. Despite it all, he perseveres. Each morning I say good-bye, tell him how much I love him and watch as he takes those thirty-five steps. When he reaches the doorway, he turns, smiles, waves and bravely enters the school.

Our father-son conversations are not about the latest in sports or how to ask that cute girl to the dance. We talk about Disney films and exotic animals. The natural world is actually quite a wonder. Instead of bragging on my son's high academic class ranking or his "lightning-quick" first step to the basket, I find myself beaming about his gifts as an artist, his near encyclopedic knowledge of animals and the pure unfiltered kindness he shows to others on a daily basis. During one of our chats, I asked him what he thought happiness was. His reply was sublimely simple: "Being nice to people and doing the best you can." I was momentarily speechless. Julian had distilled thousands of years of scholarship and thought about our very existence into an uncomplicated yet brilliant ten-word answer. I think if we all listen a little more attentively, maybe Julian and the thousands of persons like him can help make the world a better place.

Who knows, my initial plans for that trip to Norway or Sweden may not be so far-fetched, after all.

SON, YOU HAVE AUTISM

APRIL 1, 2010

Most parents spend years preparing for the "big talk" (sex) with their kids. There are strategy sessions with each other, rehearsals in front of the mirror. Sometimes props are employed; this usually raises the awkward meter. In the end, parent and child both get through it and, hopefully, there's no permanent mental scarring as they move to a new level of interaction in their relationship. But how do you tell your child he or she has autism?

Martina and I decided to tell Julian the summer between his fifth- and sixth-grade years. We realized that as he entered middle school, the social contrasts between him and his peers would become more obvious. While most kids were gravitating toward areas of interest that would be considered more traditional for adolescents—the opposite sex, popularity, the opposite sex, clothes, the opposite sex, sports, the opposite sex—Julian was happily immersed in his world of drawing, Disney, animals and mythological creatures.

The dynamics of his academic world would also begin a greater divergence from those of his peers. Though he had always been mainstreamed in school, he required special assistance in the form of extra tutors and sessions with a special needs teacher at school. A quick aside here, I want to express our family's gratitude to Ms. Karen Rodenhizer who served in that latter capacity during Julian's years in elementary school. Her combination of commitment, caring and demanding made those some of the best years of Julian's early life. The world needs more teachers like her.

With all this in mind, we sat Julian down to tell him. We began by discussing all the things that we thought were so special about him and asked him to talk about what made him really happy. As we moved to the topic of how all people are different, we showed him a couple of books about children with autism. As we explained autism and how it related to him, he became very upset. He cried, screamed, covered his ears; this was not something he wanted to hear. He put his hands up to our mouths in an attempt to silence us. This was going to be hard.

We reassured him of our love and our pride in him. Martina brought out some of his drawings, which really are quite good, and pointed out that without autism, he might not be able to create such art. He demonstrated an ability to draw before he could speak fluidly. His specialties are animals and Disney characters. We talked about his amazing recall of details about animals from around the world. All this, we told him, was a part of his autism and that we thought he was rather cool.

But all Julian "heard" was that something was wrong with him, something that couldn't be fixed. He was really concerned about who knew he had autism. This acute self-awareness is part of the nature of having high-functioning autism. He's tuned into the world around him enough to know that he is different. The majority of persons along the autism spectrum are not as high functioning as Julian. Significant numbers of those are retarded, and thus, they are more insulated in their own worlds.

At the time, we promised that only teachers and certain adults in his life would know about his autism. We wanted to allow him time to process this, something he is still doing, with a measure of success. Before seeing family members or friends, he will ask me who knows about his autism. We assured him that we foresaw a long, exciting and happy life for him. We called in Jared, his younger brother by two years, to explain this to him and talk about what it really meant to be a family, that no matter what happened, we would always stick together and be there for Julian.

Martina and I ended that emotionally taxing evening lying down on Julian's bed with him, before he went to sleep, discussing lions and Disney movies. It was a very difficult day and it would be a couple of years before he was comfortable with us even saying the word, *autism*, in his presence.

But now, at least, he knew.

Julian poses with his artwork at an art show
Courtesy of Dwayne Ballen

ARTIST IN RESIDENCE

APRIL 6, 2010

A few years ago, North Carolina and Duke were engaged in a tense and thrilling late-season men's college basketball game at Chapel Hill's Smith Center. Another memorable chapter in one of sports' fiercest rivalries was being authored as two of the nation's top ten teams waged a pitched battle before a nationally televised audience and a highly energized arena crowd. As the game entered its final nail-biting minutes, the decibel levels in the building had reached a deafening roar. All 22,000 spectators were on their feet; actually 21,999 were standing. Julian was seated, calmly focused on the small sketchpad in his lap. He was drawing Simba from the *Lion King*, his single all-time favorite character.

I gazed in amazement at my son, marveling at his ability to block out all the noise and hysteria induced by the game. He was in his own world, concentrating on his artwork. A significant number of persons with autism, especially those who (like Julian) are high functioning have something that they can do very well. Regardless of the setting or circumstance, they can dial into their "thing." This is, in part, because the nature of autism can create a laser-like attention to specific interests or subjects. In many cases, that area of concentration will dominate any discussion or interaction with that person.

When he was much younger, Julian would quickly guide any conversation to the topic of animals. He's since learned to "listen" to other people and engage them a little more, shaking their hands and inquiring about their well-being before moving on to the wonders of the Himalayan snow leopard. That may seem like people skills "101" to you, but for a person with autism, it is quite the feat. Most have no sense of traditional social interaction.

Realizing this, Martina and I have always made sure that, wherever we are, Julian has a sketchpad at his disposal so that he can go to his place of comfort. Friends and acquaintances have become accustomed to the sight of Julian sketching away. Whether it's a game, church, dining out, car trip, or a family reunion, our "artist in residence" usually has pen or pencil in hand and is creating something that brings a smile to his face and anyone around him. Not a few times, when we're out, someone within view of his sketches will strike up a conversation with him about what he's drawing. He's always happy to share and explain.

As the game neared its end, I, like the rest of the crowd, was intently watching the Tar Heels and Blue Devils go "tooth and nail" at each other when I felt a tug on my arm. I looked down and was greeted by Julian's beaming countenance. He was holding up a very detailed drawing of Simba and his friends. The pure happiness on his face was overwhelming. Suddenly, I forgot about the game.

I sat down as he told me who each character was and talked me through their relationship to each other. While over 20,000 people around him were consumed in a frenzy of college basketball, Julian had taken a trip to Pride Rock, and he'd invited me to join him.

It was a nice visit.

WHAT'S UP WITH YOUR BROTHER?

APRIL 11, 2010

Imagine how difficult it would be to learn, as a child, that you have autism and begin the long process of coming to terms with that fact. Our son Julian, who's now sixteen years of age, has been traveling that path for the last five years. His younger brother, Jared, who is fourteen, has also embarked on this journey and is still coming to terms with what it means, for him and for Julian.

"What's up with your brother?" Jared first heard those words when he was nine. The child asking the question meant nothing cruel. He simply noticed an obvious difference in Julian's behavior and the other kids playing outside that day. While the others engaged in a game of basketball, Julian remained off to the side, parallel playing, pacing back and forth, flapping his hands, laughing to himself, seemingly oblivious to the activity of the other children only a few feet away.

Jared told his playmate that Julian was okay; he wasn't interested in basketball. Later, when talking to me about the incident, Jared told me it was embarrassing for him. He was angry with Julian for drawing attention to both of them in that manner. This happened quite a bit during that stage of their lives. Despite constant efforts to explain to him that his brother wasn't intentionally trying to embarrass him and was simply doing what was natural for him, Jared's comprehension and empathy levels weren't very high. He just wanted this to stop. Martina and I understood, after all he was only nine.

During our discussions, he expressed frustration over not having a "regular" brother—one to throw a football with, one to play video games with, to do the things that most brothers do with each other. He also was tiring of (what became over the next few years) the continuous questions about Julian, from other children. Those of us with children requiring any sort of special attention must always be cognizant of the effect this has on our other children.

We talk to Jared often and have frank dialogue with him about Julian. We try to make sure that he doesn't feel there is any inequity in our family dynamic. For instance, the boys each take turns walking the dog and taking out the trash. That may seem minor, but we think it shows them that autism will not be used as an excuse not to participate in the fulfillment of family-designated responsibilities. Though Julian may need more time and a little extra help, he is always expected to do what he is asked.

As he's gotten older, Jared has developed a better understanding and appreciation for what his brother's autism means. This is a consistent topic of conversation in our house. He fully realizes Julian can no more change his autism than he can his skin color. Jared has come up with innovative ways to engage his brother, by venturing into Julian's world of interests. I watched as he once got Julian to throw a football with him as part of a challenge between Simba and Scar of *The Lion King*.

Jared continues to have times when he feels challenged and frustrated by Julian's autism, but he knows it's nothing compared to what Julian deals with on a daily basis. He even seems to handle those questions, which will never cease, from other kids with more ease. He does his best to explain autism to his peers. He also will not allow anyone to make fun of his brother. During a recent chat, he admitted to me that he has wondered what it would be like to have a different brother. I asked him would he change the circumstances if he could. His reply, after a considered pause, "Not really, because then it wouldn't be Julian and I do love my brother."

Julian (right) and brother Jared during a trip to the beach in August 2008
Courtesy of Dwayne Ballen

YOU'VE GOT A FRIEND

APRIL 16, 2010

"Jared, how do you make friends?" This was a sincere question Julian posed to his younger brother a few years ago. He was very aware of Jared's evolution into quite the social darling: a constant stream of friends beating a path to our door, invitations to middle school parties and dances, phone calls (some from girls!); you get the picture. Jared was becoming a very popular kid.

His brother's social prowess led Julian to fixate on his lack of friends, in particular at school. The heightened sense of self-awareness that some people with high-functioning autism have can be a double-edged sword when it comes to matters such as this. They realize enough to know that they are different and as any student of adolescents knows, being different is not the desire of most. We knew Julian wanted to belong.

One of the most difficult things for persons with autism—even those on the high-functioning end of the spectrum such as Julian—to do is make friends. It's not as much of an issue when they are small children. As a toddler Julian played with toys like the other kids, all of whom seemed to be occupied in their own imaginary worlds.

However, as they get older and move into adolescence, they

find it very challenging. They are not very good at reading social cues and making small talk. Martina and I watched a familiar story line play out almost yearly. Usually one or two of his classmates would attempt to befriend Julian, but they were never quite sure how to fully communicate with him, nor he with them, and the budding relationship would fizzle before it really started.

It is the rare person with autism who understands dialogue that goes beyond the literal context. In our household we are quick to let Julian know if something is said in jest. You can imagine how an inability to process that type of interaction would make it hard to "hit if off" with someone during an initial meeting. There is also the fact that many persons with autism are centered most on their own specific areas of interest and have very little curiosity for what might interest someone else.

Fortunately, Julian has been part of a social group, with four other children of similar age and autism spectrum position. It has been meeting every Friday for the past eight years. The group was started by Linda Varblow, mother of one of the participants and a professional expert in working with persons with autism. This has turned out to be one of the best things to ever happen to Julian. It has been heartwarming to watch this "band of brothers and one sister" slowly and sometimes awkwardly bond.

It wasn't easy at first. After all, they all had different areas of specific interest, but Ms. Varblow has been a model of patience and understanding. She has helped them truly learn to engage each other and think beyond their respective private worlds. They are now working on a short feature film, under the amazing guidance of independent filmmaker Todd Tinkham. The wonderful part is watching them work together and support each other. In the world of autism, this is really special! Tinkham has shepherded them from the conceptual stage to screenwriting to actual production.

Last summer, Julian participated in a six-week program known as WELL. It consisted of another small group of kids with high-functioning autism who are his age. He enjoyed the program and will continue to be involved. So, he does have friends. The other day he told me that having friends was cool. I asked specifically what was so cool about it and he told me, "Communicating."

Imagine that.

Ballen family: (from left) Jared, Dwayne, Martina and Julian, 2004
Courtesy of Dwayne Ballen

A HUG'S A WONDERFUL THING

MAY 2, 2010

The lady gave me a disapproving look. I smiled back, hopeful of conveying to her that all was fine and I wished her well as her day progressed. Julian and I were at a local market when he walked over to me, put his head on my shoulder, wrapped his arms around me and said, "I love you, Dad." I, as I usually do in this situation, returned the embrace and the sentiments. Julian, who's sixteen, is nearly six feet tall. I'm six feet two inches in height. The sight of us displaying this affection must have bothered the lady at the market. This initiation of affection from Julian happens with some regularity. While most people smile or don't react, there are those who clearly think this inappropriate. One person, upon witnessing a similar scene between Julian and me, sternly rebuked me and said, "A boy his size doesn't need to be hugging up on you like that in public."

Well, as most parents of children with autism will tell you, expressions of love and appreciation (from their children) are wonderful bonuses. A considerable portion of persons with autism are uncomfortable with any physical contact and, usually, avoid direct eye contact with others. During the earliest years of his life, Martina and I wondered if we would ever receive, without prompting, a hug from Julian. This hypersensitivity to touch, and sometimes sound, is part of an overall social withdrawal that can worsen, as a child with autism gets older.

Sometimes they may simply decide that the touch of a certain person is unappealing. I received a painfully clear education about this when Julian was around eleven. While his interaction with his mother was flowering, he wanted no part of me. He not only avoided all physical contact with me but also showed outward disdain when I would get near him physically. If I were approaching him and reached in his direction, he would frown, then turn his body to avoid me. Martina and I were baffled by this behavior, for nothing had changed in the way I treated him.

We enlisted the aid of a therapist but were never really able to get to the reason for Julian's feelings toward me, at the time. You think the mind of an adolescent is something hard to figure out, add autism to the mix. Despite being confounded by his behavior, we realized the most important thing was Julian's comfort level. So, I sat at the opposite end of the dinner table from him, tried to avoid saying too much to him, would wait until he was asleep to kiss him good night, made sure that, whenever possible, Martina would drop him off and pick him up from school, whatever it took to put him at ease.

This went on for nearly a year. I'm not going to kid you, it really hurt. Suddenly, one day when I returned home from an out-of-town trip, Julian nearly knocked me over as he ran to embrace me and tell me how much he missed me. The words do not exist to fully describe what I felt at that moment. What changed? I don't know, Martina and I still discuss that with puzzlement. I'm forever thankful that his feelings did change. Since then Julian and I have become very close.

Last week, we were standing in line at the post office when I noticed this woman staring at the both of us, her mouth wide open.

She was bowled over by the striking resemblance between the two of us. "My gosh, you're like twins!"

Julian smiled, hugged me, put his head on my shoulder and said to her, "Yes ma'am, he's my dad."

Felt pretty good to me.

A SHORT STROLL

MAY 19, 2010

I tried to occupy myself in a number of ways. Reading, that lasted for about two minutes, television, about three minutes. I sat down to work on a book I'm writing but was up from the computer before I could marshal any coherent thoughts. Nothing was working. Julian was out for a walk, alone, in our neighborhood. I watched the clock and looked out the window, clock-window, clock-window, clock-window. The beads of sweat were forming at my temples. I'm certain my body temperature rose. Had it really been just five minutes since he'd left the house?

The idea of a sixteen-year-old boy going for an afternoon stroll in what is, by most anyone's measure, a safe and friendly neighborhood would seem to be no big deal. For our family, this was a VERY big deal. It was the first time he'd actually ventured out alone. I felt especially anxious because I hadn't called Martina, who was at work, to seek her counsel before agreeing to let Julian go on his little adventure.

Independence is not something that comes easily to persons with autism, if it ever does. For most, performing day-to-day activities that you and I take for granted, is impossible without some level of assistance and/or guidance. Even persons with high-functioning autism, like Julian, need schedules and structure. We've posted a printed checklist in his bathroom to remind him he must brush his teeth, his hair, wash his face, etc.

Understand, their minds are wired completely different. I realize the same can be said about most any teenager. For Julian, the minutiae of everyday life doesn't always register. We find ourselves reminding him of, seemingly, small things: a shirt buttoned in the wrong holes or food smudges on his face after a meal. When we're away from home, I usually accompany him to the restroom, just to make sure he's okay. I tend to drift back and wait, but he knows I'm there.

When he'd asked me if he could go for a walk, my initial impulse was to go with him, but I realized this was a new step for him, seeking a measure of independence. We discussed the route he would take, by the homes of a couple of friends, and he promised to stay on the sidewalk. Of course as soon as he was out of our driveway, the aforementioned panic set in for me.

After a twenty-minute walk (three hours in dad time) he seemed especially cheery. I asked for details. Had he passed the home of a particularly close family friend? I knew he had because the sight of Julian walking prompted her to call me to make sure I was aware he was out walking, alone. He wasn't sure if he'd gone by her home or not. However, he did recall some squirrels playing, an especially colorful bird and watching an otter swim in a creek.

This all underscores the fact that Julian views the world through very different lenses, not necessarily dysfunctional, simply different. Remember he can go on in amazing detail about his animals, Disney, animated movies and mythological creatures. The walk was a success and he now takes one every day, if the weather allows. If we all could bring the passion, knowledge and joy to our endeavors that Julian has for his favorite subjects, I suspect

Julian volunteers with the WELL Program
Courtesy of the WELL Program

we'd all be a little happier and not as concerned with the smaller and less important aspects of life.

There he goes, teaching me about life, again.

YOU MUST BE A BALLPLAYER

JUNE 1, 2010

The man eyed Julian for a few moments, scanning him up and down. Wearing shorts and a T-shirt, he looked every bit the young athlete. We were waiting for our takeout order at a restaurant when the gentleman came over and, with complete confidence, made his pronouncement. "Let me guess, basketball…track…golf…heck, with those long arms, you might be a pitcher. Which is it?"

Julian, ever polite, smiled and replied, "No sir, I like to draw." It took a few moments for the stranger to process this response. After a couple of awkward moments, his mildly perplexed gaze moved from Julian to me, then back to Julian as we both smiled.

Just as I started to explain, he "got it." He smiled broadly and told Julian how wonderful it was that he liked art. He inquired about Julian's favorite subjects. Upon learning it was animals, he regaled Julian with stories of kangaroos and dingoes from a trip he had taken to the Australian Outback. As we picked up our order and departed, he encouraged Julian to never lose his passion for animals and art. He didn't have to worry on those counts.

It is human nature to do what the gentleman did—presume that this tall athletic-looking teenager must be some sort of sportsman. It happens with much more frequency now, especially when Julian is with his younger brother, Jared. Both are tall, lean and obviously growing. They do look like athletes. When this happens, Jared will quickly engage anyone about his favorite, college basketball, while Julian stands there silent with a smile. When pressed, he simply informs the inquirer that he is more into art and animals.

Julian has come quite a ways, in his response to such queries, over the past few years. Initially when someone would bring it up, he would react with confusion and a look of mild irritation. For many young children with autism, the idea of having any other pursuits, outside of their specific area of interest, is foreign, almost repellent. In his mind, especially when he was younger, the thought of venturing beyond his area of interest was a betrayal of those very interests. It was of grave concern to him if he thought someone didn't appreciate how much he loves animals. He would quickly turn to Martina or me for reassurance. "You know I love animals, right?" would be accompanied by a look of pain and worry. A simple "What sports do you play?" was all it took to get him worked up.

We continually talk with Julian about the need to recognize that people are simply being nice and "making conversation"— that phrase, of course, required another explanation. It's not literal. Remember, for most persons with autism, going beyond the literal understanding takes quite an effort over a long period of time. After years of working with him on this, Julian has now reached a point of understanding such exchanges. Just because someone asks about your jump shot, doesn't mean you don't like animals.

The incident with the gentleman in the restaurant played out again a few days ago when the boys and I ran into an old acquaintance who hadn't seen my sons in five years. He was surprised by their growth and immediately wanted to know what sports they were playing. While he and Jared began talking ACC basketball, Julian stood there with his usual wonderfully pleasant smile. I quietly asked him what he was thinking about. With a sparkle in his eyes he whispered back, "Disney's Animal Kingdom."

Somehow, I knew that.

THE WORLD'S GREATEST GIG

JUNE 17, 2010

"I got myself a caddie!" That's how I informed my close friends of the birth of Julian sixteen-and-a-half years ago. Like the game of golf we've been in the fairway, lost in the woods, had some bogeys, scrambled to make par and also aced a hole or two. This "round," as father to Julian and his younger brother, Jared, is ongoing and a joy. It's as if I'm constantly discovering new elements and nuances to the course layout known as fatherhood.

I can say with complete candor that I'm 180 degrees away from where I thought I'd be, at this stage, when Martina and I first learned of her pregnancy with Julian. I, like most fathers, had chartered the usual alpha male trek for my son before he was two months old. Boy, was I in for a real course correction. Julian's autism has forced me to view the world in a dramatically different manner. Once we received his diagnosis, at age four, I began the process of recalibrating what being a success in life meant to me. Thanks to him, I've reached a place where I understand that it's the moments and instances that most of us take for granted or give little note, that truly mark a successful life.

I went from thinking I'd never have much dialogue with my son to a sustained discussion about the subtle differences between rabbits and hares; the latter have longer ears. From him never looking me directly in the eyes to a fixed gaze as I explain to him how to make a sandwich for himself. From his avoidance of physical contact to regular embraces, initiated by him.

Life with Julian has been consistently surprising. We never know when something special is going to occur. An example of this took place on a recent evening. Following a very trying day at work, Martina and I were relaxing in our downstairs den. As we began to rehash the low points of the day, "it" cascaded down from upstairs. The sound of Julian and Jared laughing, together! We looked at each other, quickly forgot about the petty issues of that day, smiled, listened and nearly cried. This was something we thought might never happen.

Many children with autism are unable to engage their more "typical" siblings in any meaningful way. This moment was a long time in the making. Julian had to get to a point where he was willing to allow Jared entry into his world. Jared had to come to terms with the extra efforts it would take to access his brother's universe. I'm happy to report that their joint laughter has become a more familiar sound in our house.

Whether it's dressing himself, making his bed or preparing his lunch, these ordinary functions mean so much when Julian performs them. We are a long way from where we want him to be, but gosh, how far he's come in sixteen years. Yes, these things I've mentioned, for the most part, are basic and some might say simple, but for Julian, they are real achievements. So never let anyone minimize any goal you or someone you care about has reached. Julian has shown us that it's not the size or scope of the accomplishment; it's that you try and don't give up. We, as a family, celebrate all his victories, large or small. I've come to understand that fatherhood, to continue the golfing metaphors, is all about "course management." Walking the fairways with Julian and Jared make it such a special journey.

As I observe this Father's Day, it is with immense emotion, for Julian has inspired me to be a better man and given me clarity on what it means to be a father. Serving as father to Julian and Jared is definitely the best job I've ever had. Both are now lanky teenagers, but sometimes I still see my little boys when I look at them. An unknown author once wrote, "Son, you outgrew my lap, but never my heart." That says it all.

DAD, WHAT WILL MY LIFE BE LIKE?

AUGUST 20, 2010

Recently, Martina and I were having a conversation with Jared about the significance of starting high school. In a few days he will begin life as a fourteen-year-old freshman. We discussed how this period would provide the foundation for his path to college, which would, in turn, help map out his early adulthood.

Julian was not in the room at the time but, as I would later find out, he did overhear the conversation. Later that night, as I sat chatting with him in his room, he posed the question. "Dad, what will my life be like?"

Almost reflexively, I countered with "It'll be great!" That was not sufficient.

"What will I do? Will I be happy?"

For the first time that I could recall, he wanted to talk about his future.

This should've come as no surprise to me. Julian has witnessed much of our continuous dialogue with Jared regarding what he's capable of achieving, in life, if he fully prepares himself. Julian is acutely aware that we don't have the same conversations with him, at least not at the level of intensity displayed in some of our back and forth with our bright and, ahem, supremely self-confident youngest progeny.

While Jared tackles ninth-grade, Julian will continue his steady and specifically designed curriculum with an extended window for completion. He will turn seventeen later this month. He knows that many of his age peers are in full college pursuit mode. We've stressed to him that the only thing that matters is that he's happy and continues to move forward. At some point, time is not a major issue; he will get a high school diploma.

We strongly believe that there will be more education in his life beyond high school. Because of his spirit and desire to do well, I'm sure of that point. Julian knows that his autism will lead him down a less traditional path in life. That doesn't automatically mean less fulfilling or meaningful—just, as all of us who love someone with autism fully understand, different. When people ask him where he'd like to go to college, he quickly responds "Carolina." Martina works at the University of North Carolina and both of our boys have grown up on the campus. It's what they know. Naturally, Julian expects to be a student there one day. Given the high premium we place on education in our household and how much Martina and I talk to our sons about excellence, it makes sense that he would think in those terms. Who knows? Maybe Julian will make it to Chapel Hill one day as a student.

A close friend has noted several times that he thinks Julian's wondrous imagination, love of animals and ability to draw could give birth to some very enjoyable children's books. I agree and have actually asked Julian if he would like to collaborate with me on a book. He could provide illustrations and the story idea, and we could write it together. He's still thinking about it, but I sense he's warming to the idea.

So, how did I answer his other two questions that night? Well, I admit to not being prepared for his follow-ups; usually a quick enthusiastic answer of affirmation is enough to satisfy him. I asked him what would he like to do. He talked about animals, going on a safari and animated movies. I told him he already had certain gifts that would lead him to something that would make him very happy and that we would make sure he had every opportunity to succeed on his terms.

I also told him that his mother and I expected him to do well. He looked at me with a certain recognition on his face and said, "Like Jared?"

"Yes, son, just like we expect from Jared."

With a heart-stealing grin, he answered, "Cool."

Julian plays violin in his middle school's orchestral recital in December 2007
Courtesy of Dwayne Ballen

SOMETIMES IT'S JUST HARD

NOVEMBER 10, 2010

The last ten weeks have not been easy for Julian; in fact it's been a damn hard time. Without a doubt it has been the most challenging period of his young life. He suffered a mental breakdown and was hospitalized for two weeks. It was determined that the pressure he put on himself to do well in school, coupled with the increasing complexity and difficulty of his curriculum, proved to be too much for him. He simply shut down. This setback has resulted in very noticeable changes in his behavior and demeanor.

The walks through our neighborhood he used to enjoy are no longer part of his daily regimen. In fact his gait is now very slow and deliberate. His speech has changed to a pitch similar to that of a small child with the use of very few words. He no longer scours the Internet for information on animals, Disney characters and mythological creatures. His routine, upon getting home from school, is to retreat to his room with the television usually on Animal Planet while he lies on his bed clutching a well-worn stuffed Simba (from *The Lion King*), that seems to provide him with a measure of comfort. He's even stopped drawing. It's as if he's withdrawn into a world inhabited solely by Julian.

He had become so disengaged from school that we recently had to place him in a specialized school that fits a child with his specific needs. Doctors have told us that this overall apathy is not uncommon for someone recovering from a setback like the one he suffered. This new stage has required even more intense oversight of his daily routine. If I tell him to brush his teeth after dinner, he will reply, "Yes sir." Once he's upstairs I'll call after him to remind him about it, and again his reply is "Yes sir." However, it's not until I go upstairs and guide him into the bathroom to brush his teeth that the task is actually accomplished. He's not being recalcitrant; it's just the nature of where he is right now. Imagine how difficult it must be for him to have the combination of mental illness and autism.

There is one pleasant irony to this more insular Julian. Despite disconnecting from almost everything, he now wants constant hugs—not only from Martina and me but from his younger brother, Jared. The latter part of that is funny because before, Jared, like most brothers, served as a benign irritant to his brother. Martina and I would often hear refrains from Julian, "Leave me alone, Jared!" "No, Jared!" "Stop, Jared!" echoing throughout the house.

Now Julian regularly wraps Jared in long embraces and tells him he loves him. Watching Jared start to squirm, after a few seconds wrapped in these hugs, provides us with some well-needed laughter. If the "old" Julian could see the "new" Julian doing this, he wouldn't believe his own eyes. Not more than five minutes can go by, when we're with him, that Julian doesn't want to hug one of us. That is never bad.

We still do many things as a family. A couple of weeks ago, we took in the state fair, something the boys always look forward to. Actually, it's the funnel cakes and deep-fried Snickers that they really like. Julian held on to Martina's arm the entire time during our trip to the fairgrounds. She literally pulled him along as we walked. While he appears to be not nearly as involved in activities as before, we know he's taking everything in, and in his own way, enjoying it all.

We've decided to just hold on to each other, do all we can to make Julian comfortable, and get through this together, as a family.

As Martina says, "If Julian has a smile on his face, then we're moving in the right direction."

GOOD-BYE, GRANDMA KENDRICK

JANUARY 3, 2011

J ulian stared intently at his grandmother. I hadn't seen that level of focus in his eyes in quite some time. His maternal grandmother, Mrs. Ruth Kendrick, lay just a foot away from him in a hospice bed, laboring to breathe. She would end her marvelous and impactful eighty-nine years on this earth a few days later on New Year's Day. Death had visited Julian's world. It was hard to know exactly what thoughts were racing through his head at that moment. Since his setback, he hasn't been very talkative or forthcoming. It takes persistence and patience to get anything out of him. Before averting his gaze, during a five-minute study of his ailing grandmother, his brow furrowed and he mumbled something to himself.

Later, in a quasi-urgent mode, he asked Martina if he was going to die. Let's pause and be mindful of the fact that Julian is processing this in a manner none of us really understand. Remember, unless otherwise prompted or instructed, persons with autism rarely spend much time pondering matters beyond their respective realm of interest. Though we went to the funeral of a dear friend's daughter back in June, death wasn't a topic of discussion with him.

Martina's answer? She explained to Julian that he has a very long life ahead of him and went on to point out that his grandmother had lived a long time and was now at rest after a sustained illness. We're not sure if that answer satisfied him, but he didn't, voluntarily, return to the subject again. Even after we told him she had died.

I wanted to know how much of this he absorbed, so I sat with him Sunday, in his room, and gently prodded. Did he realize that he would never be able to speak with, hug or kiss his grandmother again in this life? What came to mind when he thought of her? What did he say to himself that evening at her bedside? Were there any questions he had about life and death?

Well, it probably will not surprise you to learn that Julian offered little in the way of answers. In response to what he would remember about her, he replied, "Love," simple and heartfelt. When I pressed him for more, he said, "Pork Chops." I thought that to be an odd answer until he added, "Christmas Eve." You see, his grandmother's tradition was to host a Christmas Eve dinner at her house. She always prepared an amazing meal; for Julian the pork chops stood out. Funny I don't remember the pork chops; for me it was the lamb.

Julian and his Grandma Kendrick each played a role in ushering the other into a new stage of their respective lives. When he was a toddler fidgeting in church one day, Mrs. Kendrick pulled out a piece of paper and pen and suggested to Martina that this might help occupy him until the services were over. Well, as most of you must realize, this opened the door to one of Julian's gifts, his ability to draw.

How did Julian figure in a key point of her life? Six years ago, she began showing early signs of the Alzheimer's that would eventually take her life. At that time Martina and her siblings had been discussing ways to introduce the subject to their strong-willed and fiercely independent mother. This became a regular subject in our house. That Christmas Eve, we gathered for a family picture after the aforementioned traditional dinner. As we awaited the photographer's signal, Julian, who was seated next to his grandmother, turned to her and asked, "Are you having memory problems?"

The room went completely silent; I don't think anyone even moved, except Julian. We all waited for the eruption. What seemed like minutes were only a few seconds. She knew full well that his autism didn't provide him with much of a filter, and this was something he'd overheard. So she looked at her grandson, cocked her head to one side, smiled and replied, "Well, buddy, I guess I am." Why he asked that question at the moment is a mystery. But he did and the topic became easier to bring up as Mrs. Kendrick and her family began what has been aptly called the "long goodbye."

As for his grandmother's passing, I think, somehow, Julian, understands and comprehends what has happened. Maybe that evening, as he sat near her, in his own way he was saying goodbye.

SHAKE YOUR GROOVE THING, JULIAN

FEBRUARY 21, 2011

Jared was in the middle of the dance floor displaying his impressive dance skills with an energetic performance of The Dougie. Ask the nearest teenager; he or she will educate you. Julian was standing in the rear of the room with his mom. This was a birthday party for the son of two of our close friends. Martina and I, being the cool (wink-wink) adults we are, were asked to serve as chaperones for the party. I sat in a dark corner, which is where all chaperones live at such affairs, with the birthday boy's father, my friend Reggie. My gaze was back and forth—between Jared's moment of social glory and Julian's distance, socially and physically, from the reveling teenagers on the dance floor.

While hip-hop music was blaring from the sound system, all I could hear, as I looked at my eldest son, was that 1970s searing paean to teenage awkwardness, "At Seventeen" by Janis Ian. There he stood: handsome, well-mannered, considerate, socially disconnected, watching from the sidelines as his fellow teenagers celebrated with dance. Being a teenage is hard enough, autism doesn't help.

My seventeen-year-old son stood there and I hurt for him, longing for a magic wand to wave and turn him into another fun-loving teenager at the party. As my tear ducts started to open up, I turned away to try and compose myself. At that moment, Reggie tapped me on the shoulder to draw my attention back to Julian. He was dancing! Martina was right there with him as they turned the refreshment area into, in my mind, the home of the spotlight dance.

Julian was performing a choreographed hip-hop routine he'd learned two summers ago during a wonderful six-week program (WELL) for teenagers with high-functioning autism. He had fully committed the routine to memory. Despite the difficulties he's had recently, because of his regression, he was the picture of precision. The hand gestures, the slides, the head bob, he had it all down. On top of all that, he was smiling. Julian was having fun!

Though many, previously ordinary, functions had become a challenge for Julian, he was able to recall and execute that dance routine, with the attendant enthusiasm. All it took was prompting from Martina. This reminded me of the sometimes mysterious and amazing quality of the mind of a person with autism. A study conducted at Ohio State University concluded that, in certain circumstances, persons with high-functioning autism have better memory performance and higher memory capacities than the rest of us. I suspect continued research into autism will eventually help us better understand new ways to tap into the potential of the human brain.

Meanwhile, back at the dance, led by Martina and our friend Ranota, Julian had found his way to the dance floor. There he was amid the rest of the kids dancing, beaming and shaking his groove thing. You go, son.

MOM, DAD, LOOK AT THIS!

MARCH 16, 2011

J ulian stared at the picture of the leopard and began to smile. We were visiting a bookstore when the picture book, featuring big cats of the wild, caught his eye. "Hey Dad, I want that book." This was the first time since last summer that he had initiated real dialogue or shown any significant interest in anything. He had socially, verbally and emotionally retreated to the point that rare was the circumstance when we could engage him in any activity or conversation.

Pleasantly surprised, I quickly started in with the questions. What about the book caught his attention? What could he tell me about the leopard on the cover? How were leopards different from cheetahs? They looked the same to me. He responded in rapid-fire fashion, with certainty and a strong voice. Cheetahs have longer legs, smaller heads and are much faster than leopards. In fact they are the world's swiftest land animals, reaching speeds of up to 75 miles per hour. They can go from 0 to 64 miles per hour in three seconds. All this was tumbling out of Julian. Had our Rip Van Winkle awoken from his prolonged sleep? I was overcome with joy. Julian was back!

Over the past few weeks, we've watched as his old interests resurfaced. Animal Planet, Disney movies and mythological creatures, yes, the old gang is back together. He even has begun drawing again. The interesting thing is that after a dormant period of nearly eight months, he seems to have retained his artistic ability and nearly encyclopedic knowledge of animals. Recently, I asked him to draw a detailed scene of the Serengeti, one of his favorite places on earth. Though he'd done this in the past, I expected there to be a bit of hesitancy. After all, he hadn't held a pen to draw since mid-summer. At the very least, I anticipated he would need to see a picture to jog his memory. No reminders were necessary.

The drawing flowed out of him as if he had been doing it every day without pause. The detail was impressive. Watching him work from memory with such care and detail made me think of Stephen Wiltshire, the young man with autism who drew an intricate picture, eighteen feet wide, of the New York City skyline after viewing it one time during a twenty-minute helicopter ride.

It underscores what the International Society of Autism Research has determined is "the greater long-term retention of memory for details" that some people with autism possess. Julian is living proof. Despite that sustained period of detachment, he is quick to recall specifics about his areas of interest. It's as if this storehouse of information has been slumbering inside him all this time, waiting for Julian to allow it to come out of hibernation.

Naturally, there are questions that we don't have answers to. What triggered his re-engagement with the external world? I have no idea. Maybe his therapist will help shed some light on that, but the most important thing is that our son is laughing, drawing and talking again. All is not perfect; we continue to deal with other challenges, some new, that he faces. Seeing those beautiful eyes sparkle with curiosity and a newfound sense of happiness is enough to fortify Martina and me as this special journey continues with our wondrous son. He's even back on the computer, daily, searching for information on animals, and he wants to share. There are now nightly shouts from the office where he conducts his Internet searches, "Mom, Dad, come look at this!"

Few things have ever sounded better to me.

HURTING FOR MY SON

Earlier in this book, I alluded to Julian's breakdown; allow me to go into more detail. This was and remains a very painful place for me to venture, but with the benefit of distance and perspective, I'm prepared to revisit what was a very difficult period for our family. I wish for no one to ever have to experience this with his or her child. It altered Julian's developmental trajectory and we are (still) dealing with the residual effects.

After a challenging but ultimately successful freshman year of high school, Julian began his tenth-grade year at the Durham (NC) School of the Arts with the promise of another step forward in his educational journey. However, we quickly began to realize that this would be a difficult year. The workload required for his course of study (college prep) overwhelmed him, and it proved increasingly difficult for him to keep up with the pace and requirements of the curriculum.

During considerable consultation with DSA Assistant Principal Willa Sample, who had become Julian's biggest champion and shepherd at the school, we came to the conclusion that another formula might be the best way to advance Julian's education and, more importantly, make him more comfortable. We decided upon a plan that would have him spend the first part of his day at DSA and the second half at The Hill Center, a Duke University connected center that provides specialized instruction in intimate classroom settings.

So, every day, I would pick Julian up during the late morning and transport him across town to the Hill Center. While there, his instruction featured classes with a maximum of four students per teacher. Martina and I felt we have hit upon the right combination for Julian; he would maintain his connection to DSA where his imagination and talent for drawing could flower while the smaller learning environs at the Hill Center, hopefully, would allow him to absorb the information easier, with the guidance of a more hands-on instructor.

A couple of months into this routine, Julian began to show signs of increased tension. Since he and I spent so much time together, I was hopeful of getting him to open up to me about what was bothering him. During our daily trips home from the Hill Center, I tried to engage him as much as possible, but he was becoming more withdrawn. He slowly became less verbal. His progress, whatever he had made to that point, at the Hill Center went into complete reverse.

It turns out that the smaller classroom was a bigger problem. Julian was the first child with autism they'd admitted to the Hill Center. Most of the other students had learning challenges of varying degrees but none had autism. Being in such close proximity to only a couple of other students and the teacher only highlighted Julian's awareness of his differences. Thus, the familiar nature of Julian's high-functioning autism. He's acutely aware that he's not like the other kids. Sitting next to students who were making clear progress, while he wasn't, simply made him more tense and heightened his anxiety levels. Despite all the best intentions of the teachers at the Hill Center, it wasn't working.

The holiday season was rapidly approaching and it was our hope that the break would reenergize Julian. Christmas is Julian's favorite time of the year. He loves holiday music; not a few times have I walked by his room during the dog days of summer and heard the sounds of Vanessa Williams' Christmas CD cooling the early August weather. He gets absolutely giddy at the idea of finding a new Disney movie DVD under the tree. He enjoys the decorations, the family gatherings; he loves it all.

Despite the backdrop of his favorite time of year, Julian went into full retreat mode. He began to pause while walking, literally stopping in his tracks for (apparently) no reason. When he would come to these freezes, he frequently stared off into space. It was as if he was "checking out" for the moment. Verbally, he began to shut down. Full sentences were replaced by one-word answers and his voice took on the pitch of a small child. Prior to the holiday break, Ms. Sample had begun to notice some of this at school, but now the reversal was starkly dramatic.

Julian, who loves food, stopped eating. Martina or I would sit with him, pleading and cajoling in the hopes that he eat even the most minor portions. He would lose twenty pounds over a two-month period because of this loss of appetite. It was especially obvious that Christmas Day in 2009 during our annual holiday dinner at home. Seated at the dining room table with close family friends Cricket Lane and Jeff Eisen, I sat close to my sixteen-year-old son; attempting to get him to eat and speak, to no avail. I could tell by the look on Cricket's and Jeff's faces that they were stunned by the obvious physical and behavioral changes in Julian.

One week later, we were in the car headed down to Pinehurst, NC to visit Martina's mother when we made the decision to take Julian to the emergency room at the University of North Carolina Medical Center. He was rapidly getting worse. Staring at his hands and indicating that he was seeing colors, he was also now hearing voices. During an examination by the attending physician, Julian was unable to produce a simple drawing of a cat. Something he previously did with ease and speed. His responses to the doctor's questions were no more than minimal utterances. He would, unprompted, stand up and simply start shaking his arms as though he were trying to loosen some invisible force that had taken hold of him. Something was clearly wrong. The doctor immediately checked Julian into the hospital. For the next two weeks, my son would be a patient in the children's psychiatric ward.

The first night was hard. Other than trips to visit his grandmothers, Julian had never spent a night away from home without either Martina or me with him. The staff could not have been more considerate and kind. We were allowed to stay with Julian until he was comfortably in bed and drifting off to sleep. I stood over his bed, holding his hand, as his eyelids got heavier. My son was in a different place, literally and figuratively, and I felt hopeless. All I could do was hurt for him. Leaving his room late that night was one of the hardest things I've ever done.

Each morning, I was there to wake him up and get him dressed. Fortunately, the hospital was a few hundred yards from Martina's office, so one of us was with him every moment the hospital allowed. Having autism is one thing, adding mental illness to the equation is almost unbearable. I watched my son go through his own form of hell over the next ten days. For Martina and me, there was the unsettling thought that this might be it; maybe Julian would never recover. Each evening, Martina, Jared and I would visit with Julian. I know this was not easy for Jared, watching the brother he knew undergo this radical change for the worst. He asked me if Julian would ever be okay. Would we always have to visit him in a hospital? Why was this happening? Honest and understandable questions from a confused fourteen-year-old.

The support of relatives and friends provided immeasurable comfort to us during this time. Cricket Lane and Ranota Hall, two very close family friends, were regular visitors. One night, as we were visiting with Julian, Cricket said to Martina, "That's not our Julian, but he's in there, somewhere. This will not last." Ms. Kathleen Wright, who has been a teacher, tutor and so much more to Julian, made special trips to see him. The mention of her name always brings a smile to his face. She is one of those people who has a special sense and feeling when it comes to interaction with persons on the autism spectrum. There also were regular telephone calls for Julian. My mom, Martina's brother, Scott; and sister, Pam; my Uncle Harold and Aunt Pearl, whom I'm especially close to, all called to let him know how much he was loved.

The doctors tried a combination of medications before settling on a cocktail that was beginning to produce positive results. This was new territory for us. Julian had never been on any type of medication. It was something we, well, actually I, resisted for a long time. Early in the second week, Julian began to show signs of improvement. When the doctors examined him, they would offer encouraging words. "Julian, you look good. You're doing great!"

Julian took these words to heart and they now have become a regular part of our discourse with him. He routinely asks Martina and me how he looks. For him this is a way of confirming he's okay and doing well. Not a day goes by that Julian does not pose the question to one of us: "Dad, how do I look?" His face always lights up when he hears the positive response.

Upon his release from the hospital, Julian returned to the Durham (NC) School of the Arts with a modified schedule. It didn't take us long to realize that this wasn't going to be the best place for him. In his still delicate state, the rigors, despite the altered course load, of attending a large public school were counterproductive. We were fortunate to find a small alternative school that fit Julian's needs. He now attends, and is flourishing at, the Lakeview Therapeutic Learning Center.

The road back from his breakdown has been long and continues. Initially, while he no longer heard voices, he still wasn't too verbal and required constant care for the most elemental functions of everyday life. But we are so happy that he has improved to the point that he is productive at school, getting A's and B's, drawing again and full of dialogue about his beloved animals and Disney movies. Our friend Ranota Hall, who is also a highly respected child psychiatrist, told us that a full recovery, if it ever comes, will take a long time. That's fine with us; he has come such a long way from where he was.

Besides, the sight of his smile and sound of his laugh are amazing cure-alls.

TANTRUMS AND THINGS

I could sense the frustration in Martina's voice. I listened and tried to be understanding and consoling. Julian, who was three-and-a-half at the time, had thrown a major tantrum. He'd completely wrecked his room and it took Martina most of the evening to restore calm. This had become a common occurrence. Julian was not very verbal and had difficulty expressing himself with words, so he would act out his exasperation with loud and sometimes violent fits. He had yet to be diagnosed with autism, so we weren't sure what was going on. Martina and I wondered if we were witnessing a rare, sustained and intense extension of the "terrible twos." We didn't know what was driving our son's frequent flights into the world of tantrums.

This period was compounded by the fact that I spent most of my time away from home. When Julian was one, I left my job as a local sports anchor, for the ABC affiliate in the Raleigh-Durham (N.C.) market to become an anchor for The Golf Channel, based in Orlando. I traveled home on weekends. Two years later, I moved on to the Fox Sports Network, again as an anchor, which was based in Los Angeles. As was the case with The Golf Channel, I traveled home two days a week, which was barely enough time to readjust to the change of time zones.

So, as I traversed the country as a sports anchor, it was up to Martina to deal with handling two small children—one of whom was acting out in ways we could not understand. She did have help from our nanny, Gayle Stephens. Gayle was tremendous. She joined us when Julian was born and remained in our employ until both boys were enrolled in school. Gayle would often take the brunt of Julian's tantrums during the day, while Martina was at work.

However, each day at five, when Martina would return home from her demanding job as Chief Financial Officer of athletics at the University of North Carolina, Gayle would leave. This meant that Martina would go from a full and taxing day of work right into a full and extremely trying evening with Julian. He was not too verbal at the time and was unable to tell you why he was upset. This really wore her down.

So it was with a sense of empathy and longing to be there to help her that I quietly listened as she recapped that night's episode with Julian. On this particular evening, she had come home to find that Gayle had removed nearly all his toys, wall hangings, books and pictures from sight. His room was pretty much bare, with the exception of his bed. Earlier in the day, Julian had ripped pictures down from the walls, knocked over most his pictures and had thrown his toys all over the room. Gayle, not knowing what else to do, simply removed from his sight any objects that he could throw or destroy.

That's what Martina came home to most nights. And I wasn't there. As she spoke, the contrast in our current situations was clear. She was home, doing all the "heavy lifting," while I spent my time in Los Angeles doing a nationally televised nightly sports show. My routine was simple and easy. I would leave my Burbank hotel room each morning and head to the Hollywood YMCA to work out.

The place was always full of film and television stars of varying levels. I played basketball with the likes of Denzel Washington and George Clooney. Often, when I was home on the weekends, I would point out persons in commercials, films or television shows that I had just talked to at the gym that week. After my daily workouts, it was off to work on the Fox lot.

There the differences in my daily routine and Martina's became even greater. I had a dressing room with a suit of clothing (to be worn on the air that evening) already laid out by our head of wardrobe. Fox had a deal with Donna Karan to provide the on-air talent with clothing. There was a "green room" just for talent that had food and beverages selected especially for us, someone was assigned to come around every day and find out what I wanted to eat that day. There was even a barber, on site, to provide weekly haircuts. Before going on the air each evening, I had to go into makeup. There were at least two persons attending my colleagues and me, in these sessions, at all times.

So with that in mind, you can understand how a slight disconnect began to develop between Martina and me. She never got a break and my whole experience in Los Angeles was centered on me. My weekly schedule was to catch the red-eye flight home on Thursday evening/Friday morning. I would spend less than seventy-two hours at home before Martina and the boys would take me back to the airport on Sunday mornings, to catch my return flight to Los Angeles. I had to be on the air on Sunday evenings. This was every week, four weeks a month. Twenty-five thousand flight miles per month. This is not something I would recommend to anyone.

One Sunday as I was exiting the car and saying my usual good-byes to my family, I attempted to kiss Julian and he turned away from me. He was not happy that Daddy was leaving, again! Jared, who was an infant, smiled and giggled when I kissed him.

I knew things had to change. As it turned out, executives at Fox changed things for me. Later that year, there was a turnover in management, and as is normally the case in these situations, the new bosses made changes. I was one of those changes. My contract wasn't renewed and I was now free to return home to my family.

I was now able to engage my family fully. Though I would work with various networks, such as CBS Sports, ESPN and Fox Sports Net, in a freelance capacity over the subsequent years, my family—in particular Julian and Jared—would command most of my attention and energy. This would turn out to be a blessing. It was shortly after my return as a "full-time" father that Julian was diagnosed with autism.

The tantrum that was the topic of my conversation with Martina during that earlier referenced telephone conversation turned out to be the beginning of a long line of outbursts, some violent, from Julian. Before he was fully verbal, they appeared to be born from his frustration over being unable to express himself. Later, as he developed language and became fully capable of verbal interaction, those tantrums continued and sometimes were quite ugly and alarming.

When he reached his adolescent years, the frequency of these outbursts increased. It seemed that any small thing could set Julian off—whether it was my correcting him on what seemed to be a minor matter or his not receiving the proper response, to a question, from Martina or me. If he thought we were upset with him, he would then become the aggressor, attempting to force a confrontation.

One pattern that became very disturbing for Martina and me would occur while we were in a vehicle with Julian. I picked him up from school one day—he was thirteen at the time—and he had not done well on an assignment. As I asked him about this, he became increasingly angry and grabbed my arm as I was driving, causing the car to swerve. I quickly pulled to the side of the road. I was angry and shocked. What was he thinking? My anger with him didn't help the situation; he simply responded by escalating his actions. So, I took a deep breath, relaxed and spoke softly to him about how dangerous a thing he had just done was, to both of us.

Thinking he was calm, I got back on the road and continued to talk with him about what had just happened. His anger intensified again. This time he opened the passenger door, while the car was moving, threatening to jump out. I was now scared and quickly pulled to the shoulder and parked. I never could calm him down completely and had to drive the rest of the way home with the child safety locks in place on the car. Unfortunately, Martina and I, both separately and together, witnessed scenes like this multiple times over the next couple of years.

He also went through a phase, about this same time, that saw him attack me physically. One incident will always stay with me. It happened when he was fourteen. I was downstairs preparing dinner for the boys. Earlier, I'd asked Julian to put his school things away; they were strewn about the kitchen where he'd dropped them upon arriving home from school. He was upstairs in his room, lost in his world of animals and Disney. After no response from a couple of my reminders, I, losing my patience at this point, shouted up to him to come down right away and gather his things.

Upon hearing my voice, Julian knew I was not happy with him. He quickly came downstairs and began picking up his books and bag, but he fixated on me. He began to repeat that he was sorry. I said, "Just do what I asked you to do." Unhappy with my response, he forgot about his school items and zeroed in on me. Beyond the rapidly repetitive "I'm sorrys," and despite my continually telling him it was okay and reminding him that I simply wanted him to listen, Julian lost it. In his mind, I hadn't given him an adequate response, so his way of dealing with this was to go on the offensive.

First, he grabbed me as he continued to say he was sorry. I told him not to do that, it didn't matter. As he continued to grab and squeeze my arms, I grabbed him and told him to stop. He then had a rage in his eyes that I hadn't seen before. He yelled, "I hate you!"

By that time, he had pulled away and balled his fists as if to fight me. I, having gotten quite angry, shouted back, "Are you crazy?! What's wrong with you? I'm your father!" I told him to go to his room, he said no and tried to kick me. I blocked the kick, and in a manner of seconds, had him in a bear hug. While I held him, he swung at me several times shouting, all the while, about how he wished I were dead. Finally realizing he couldn't overpower me, Julian began to calm down. I sent him to his room but was very disturbed by what had just transpired. What caused my son to snap like that? How did I help or hurt the situation? Was this going to become common?

Incidents like this did happen again, not a few times. There was even the added dimension of him telling us he wished he were dead and threatening to kill himself. One time, with Martina, he raced into the kitchen and reached for a knife, indicating that he would use it on himself. This prompted us to go through a period where all knives were removed from countertops and hidden in different parts of the kitchen.

I should note that while Martina witnessed these outbursts, Julian never physically attacked her. After each of these episodes,

Julian, after cooling off, has always been very contrite. He will come to us telling us how much he loves us and is so sorry for his actions. But he can never tell us why he erupted. Though the violence has reduced dramatically, Julian still has emotional outbursts that reveal a level of anguish about his life that leaves Martina and me confused and crying.

Over the years, we've sought the counsel of a number of therapists. Currently, he sees Dr. Lin Sikich, a nationally renowned expert in the field of autism and mental illness, at the University of North Carolina. She has been wonderful in getting Julian to open up more about his anxieties regarding having autism, his family and his overall thoughts about his life. He looks forward to his bimonthly visits with her. In fact the mention of her name brings a smile to his face.

Dr. Sikich's sessions have revealed to us that Julian never intends to inflict harm (emotional or physical) on any of us, but that sometimes he has a very difficult time of truly identifying what is bothering him and, once he has recognition, how to express it or talk about the issue. We know he loves us and there are many more days filled with hugs, smiles and laughter than there are with stress and tears. At eighteen he has some of the same obstacles he had when he was first diagnosed at age four; foremost among those is how to properly communicate with the world around him. Some things may never change; that's autism.

If you or someone you care about is touched by autism, and chances are that's the case with most everyone, please remember that you can't use traditional parameters when it comes to understanding and dealing with that person. You must always be mindful that as frustrating as the interaction is for you, it is often taking a greater toll on the person with autism.

APRIL 24, 2011-OCTOBER 20, 2011

Julian and brother, Jared, at Disney World in 2008
Courtesy of Dwayne Ballen

THE MAGICAL BAG

I recognized the familiar facial expressions, however subtle, as the lady approached. Her face was covered with befuddlement accompanied by a small measure of disapproval. Julian, unaware of her at first, was blissfully engrossed with the items in his hands. A toy zebra and a large gift bag covered with Disney characters, a very large bag! We had just visited a toy store, as promised to Julian for doing so well recently, where his face lit up at the sight of the bag.

While Martina and Jared ventured inside another retail store, Julian and I waited outside, enjoying the soothing, spring afternoon weather. I was seated on a bench; he stood in front of me. By the time the previously referenced woman was upon us, Julian had greeted her with a hello and that heart-melting, ear-to-ear smile that I've come to love so much. He then proudly held up the bag and began to explain which character came from which Disney animated movie.

At this point, the transformation was complete in the woman, who'd paused her shopping day for a brief chat with Julian. She was now mesmerized, smiling and listening intently. From the earlier distance, all she saw was a physically typical, seventeen-year-old boy holding, and transfixed by, a toy animal and a small child's gift bag. To her initial gaze, I imagine, the scene appeared "off," hence the very noticeable immediate facial reaction of disapproval.

It only took a matter of seconds for her to see the genuine joy that those items brought Julian and the alacrity with which he was willing to share information about Disney and animals. As their short visit ended, she told Julian that her favorite Disney animated film was *Snow White*. He then told her that one fell under the category of "Classics," whereas his favorite, *The Lion King*, was under the heading of "Renaissance." Who knew?! Julian did. As she walked away, she paused, turned and with complete sincerity said, "Julian, it was REALLY nice to meet you."

That encounter emphasizes something Martina and I have come to terms with as Julian's parents. Allowing him to have the things that bring him comfort and joy whenever he wants them, no matter the circumstance or setting. There was a time, as he moved into his teenage years, that we restricted where and when he could carry toys and other items we deemed age inappropriate. We did not want people giving "those looks" or making fun of him in public. Frankly, there were moments when it could be a little embarrassing.

Well, we were wrong. These things, toy animals and all things Disney, make Julian happy. They represent the center of his universe—not ours, "his." Given all that he has dealt with in his seventeen years, he deserves the measure of comfort these items bring him.

The day we got the bag Jared opted to remain in the car, listening to his iPod, while we went into the toy store. When we returned to the car, an excited Julian showed Jared the bag. Jared's response? "What's in it?" Nothing, it was empty. Julian's unbridled glee derived from the simple possession of a bag with some of his most cherished characters featured on the outside. Realizing this, Jared smiled and said, "That's cool, Julian." That's all the validation Julian needed. He then became lost in a delightful world of his own entire making.

So when we're out and people give us those looks, we simply respond with smiles. It rarely takes long, after seeing Julian, for them to "get it." Truth is, it really wouldn't matter if they did or not. To paraphrase Jared, if it's cool with Julian, it's cool with us.

That's how we roll.

DAD, ABOUT GIRLS...

MAY 28, 2011

Julian and I were seated at the kitchen counter eating lunch and discussing Disney animated characters. Actually, he was giving me a tutorial on the different villains featured in these movies. It is his considered opinion that Scar (*The Lion King*) and Frollo (*The Hunchback of Notre Dame*) are far and away the most diabolical. Then, seemingly out of nowhere, he posed a question. "Dad, will I have a girlfriend?" Okay, I didn't see that one coming.

Maybe it shouldn't have surprised me; he is a seventeen-year-old boy. By nature, most are consumed with thoughts of the fairer, and at that age far smarter, sex. Though I've long since had "the talk" with him, and periodically inquire about his interest in girls, it isn't something that comes up much. I spend a lot of time with my two sons and we talk about everything. Jared, who is fifteen, constantly peppers me with queries about, among other things, girls. Though Julian doesn't offer much on the topic, I now realize he's taking it all in.

Girls do notice him. Recently, during a visit to a shopping mall, we were in a clothing store that's frequented by teenagers. Martina wanted to pick up a few things for the boys. I assumed my customary position in these scenarios: muted support, nodding

approval when signaled by Martina and pretending to understand Jared's curious fashion choices. While Julian was educating
me on the Set animal (Egyptian mythology) and happily going
on about its mysteries, a few racks over, a young lady was staring
at him. He had no clue.

She worked her way over to the rack nearest us and a made a
point of smiling and saying hello, giving Julian one of those very
friendly looks. He smiled and waved, as he does with everyone,
and quickly returned to Egyptian mythology. I found the irony
both touching and humorous. Despite standing right next to him,
she still would have to travel quite a distance to reach Julian's
world.

I don't think she ever noticed the small animal figure clutched
in his hand. She just saw a cute boy and wanted to get his attention. After she walked away, I asked him if he realized she was
flirting with him. Of course I knew the answer. Persons with
autism rarely are able to pick up on social language and cues. He
thought she was being polite and saying hello. So, with that in
mind, hopefully, you can better understand why I was caught
off-guard when he presented me with the question about his
future with girls.

However, this was an opportunity to draw something out of
him, so I went for it.

"Would you like to have one?"

"Maybe, someday."

"What kind of girl would she be?"

"Someone who likes my interest." In a very deliberate manner,
he used his fingers to denote each one.

"Disney, animals, cryptozoology, animated movies and R&B
music."

"I'm sure when the time is right, you'll meet her."

"Okay, thanks, Dad."

At that moment I didn't know whether to cry or smile. I want so much for Julian to experience the full breadth of life and, if possible, to know the kind of love his mom and I share. It will take an extremely special person to connect with him on that level; it will not be easy. Not impossible, but not easy. The good thing is that we have plenty of time to help him prepare to navigate that world. Remember, he's seventeen and in no hurry.

Martina and I have now begun planning for ways to place him in safe social settings where he can interact with girls of his age and understanding. His favorite musical artists are, in no certain order, Alicia Keys, The Temptations, Jill Scott, Al Green and Earth, Wind & Fire. Whoever the young lady is that hopes to win Julian's heart she must be open to his love of animals, animated films, mythological creatures and Disney, plus his taste in music.

Because as EW&F might put it, that's the way of Julian's world.

MOST IMPROVED STUDENT

JUNE 7, 2011

"Are you going to make it to the awards ceremony?" The voice posing the question was that of Ms. Janice Cherry, one of the administrators at Julian's school. I hadn't given it much thought. It was early June, the final day of school (one with an early release) and I was simply calling to let them know I'd have to get him out even earlier because of a doctor's appointment. My day was already full, but Ms. Cherry's benign forcefulness convinced me that I should attend the ceremony.

I arrived a couple of minutes before the presentation began and settled into a seat just before Julian and his classmates filed into the room. This is a small, specialized school with a total student body that fluctuates between twenty-five to thirty. My eyes met Julian's the moment he entered the room. While we exchanged smiles and waves, I took stock of my eldest son who, at seventeen years of age, had been through more than many do by middle age.

About five feet nine inches in height with a slender build, Julian has one of the most pleasant bearings of anyone I've ever known. Handsome with full eyebrows and a smile that starts in his eyes and winds down to his mouth, he is warm and open to the world. He is quick to say hello and always utilizes "yes, ma'am" and "yes, sir" when speaking to adults. A more respectful child, you will never meet.

All the school's teachers joined Ms. Cherry at the front of the room as she opened the program by welcoming everyone, then got right to the matters at hand. "We're going to go out of order because one of the students we're recognizing today has to leave early. Julian, would you please come forward?" With that request Julian sprang to his feet and bounded to the front of the room while looking back at me and smiling. I, completely surprised, glanced at Ms. Cherry as she gave me a knowing nod. Good thing I had listened to her subtle suggestion about attending.

She announced that Julian had been selected to receive two honors, most improved and most respectful. As each teacher took turns with brief words about Julian, I choked up as I watched and listened. He had traveled quite a figurative distance since arriving at the school in January.

When the teachers and administrators at the Lakeview Therapeutic Learning Center first met him, Julian was still suffering the residual effects of his breakdown and was a shell of his former self. He spoke in a soft, toddler-like whisper, he wouldn't hold a pen or pencil to write on his own, and he'd lost his appetite. Julian dropped twenty-one pounds from his slight frame during this period. He actually required the care one would give a child just learning to walk and talk.

The amazing and highly dedicated staff was undaunted by this. They took Julian in, determined that he would emerge much better. They had no reference points, as we did, about what Julian was like or could do. It probably seemed a bit like fantasy as Martina and I described the old Julian: his drawing, love of animals, love of discussion of animals, the spark for life. But they took our words to heart, and with patience and whatever form of encouragement necessary, have helped guide our son back from what Martina has called a very dark place.

As I basked in the glow of my son's accomplishment, I looked at him with sincere admiration. What an example of fortitude and desire. No matter how bad things were, we always knew, deep down, Julian wanted to get better. Ralph Waldo Emerson wrote, "We acquire the strength we overcome."

Boy, did Julian look mighty strong standing at the front of that classroom.

FATHER TO FATHER

His face was a mixture of mild uncertainty and anticipation. Andrew, a new acquaintance, was asking me about my experience with Julian and Jared. Like me he has two sons, about two years apart in age. The eldest, as is the case in our family, has autism. The difference is Andrew's sons are much younger than my teenagers, Julian and Jared, who are now seventeen and fifteen, respectively. Was there any insight I could offer on what lies ahead for him as a father?

Flexibility was the first word that came to mind. I recalled that Julian's autism forced me to recalibrate my view of, what most would consider to be, the traditional father-son dynamic. I had to accept that it was unlikely he and I would re-create a Norman Rockwell-inspired image of the father teaching the son the nuances of throwing a curve ball and a slider. I had to get to a place of understanding that Julian was not going to grow up to be a man of (traditional) power, astride the worlds of business and philanthropy like a colossus, as I originally expected of any son of mine. Bottom line, Julian was going to show us the pathway of his life's journey.

I suggested to Andrew that his son would provide their family with unforeseen moments of joy that will leave indelible impres-

Julian enjoys the antics of a gorilla at a North Carolina zoo in 2007
Courtesy of Dwayne Ballen

sions. He will take them places they never expected to venture. Julian has opened up the world of animals and Disney to a degree that I never would've imagined. His gifts as an artist have truly moved me. He and I visited a local zoo recently and watching the pure delight he took in looking at the animals reminded me that there are myriad ways to experience happiness.

I also had to be honest with Andrew. There will be trying times. Challenges you can't imagine. There have been occasions when I've gotten quite upset with Julian. Despite being well aware of the fact, I've had to remind myself that Julian's brain functions differently and he doesn't "see" things the way most of us do. Yes, having a child with autism can be frustrating and even heartbreaking at times, for even the most patient of parents. It's human nature.

There are times Julian does things, which he shouldn't, that have little to do with autism and everything to do with being a kid, or worse, a teenager! We've found that letting him know he has to meet the same standard of respectful behavior and conduct, as his brother, has been a plus in his development.

There will be larger issues that arise that you simply have to summon the courage to battle. We've learned that with Julian's educational and social challenges. It's a hard thing to listen to an educator tell you there is no place for your child at their school.

I shared with Andrew that he should guard against being overly punitive with the neurotypical son. I've been guilty of this with Jared. Because "he should know better," sometimes I've been especially hard on him, in stark contrast to dealing with Julian on the same issue. What all of us, parents of siblings of children with autism, should be aware of is that it can be very difficult for those children who are growing up with a brother or sister who demands such special attention and understanding.

What I am hopeful of more than anything else is that Andrew came away from our conversation feeling optimistic and excited about the voyage he and his family have embarked upon. It is a wonder, watching the child with autism make an imprint on all others around them. And watching the other child develop and gain a greater appreciation for all persons and things that are "different" in our world.

At the end of our visit, Andrew's face seemed a bit more relaxed and calm. Maybe being able to share thoughts with someone who's a bit farther down this road of autism and parenting helped. There was one final thought I wanted to leave with him. Through all of this, you will emerge a better man and father; I certainly hope that I have. That daily striving for improvement never stops; Julian makes sure of that.

After all, isn't trying to be better every day one of the real keys to fatherhood.

THE MEASURE OF A
YOUNG MAN

AUGUST 7, 2011

Recently, our family attended a celebration/sendoff for the son of two of our dearest friends. The young man was headed off to college. Family and close friends gathered for an evening of dining, dancing and joy. Julian and our friends' son are in the same age range, so for us this was a real reminder of Julian's autism and the different trek we are embarked upon with him.

While everyone congratulated the young man and participated in the joy of the occasion, I watched Julian to gauge his reaction to this event. Julian will enter eleventh grade this fall while the evening's honoree is headed to a prestigious university on an academic scholarship. Julian has known the college-bound lad his entire life. They were playmates as toddlers. We have a picture of the two of them enjoying juice boxes and sharing a wagon ride when they were both still in Pampers.

I did not want Julian to feel he wasn't measuring up in comparison to our friends' son. When they saw each other, Julian gave him a handshake and a hug while congratulating him on his scholarship. May I be allowed a sidebar here? To see Julian continue to evolve like this and interact with people, considering where he was only eight months ago is so heartwarming and inspiring.

Following their exchange, I checked in with Julian.

"What do you think, buddy?"

"It's nice."

"Anything you want to talk about?"

"Uh…no, sir. Well, how am I doing, Dad?"

"Great and we're so proud of you."

"Thanks, Dad!"

Julian was good. He just needed to know that, in our judgment, he was doing well. He did not dwell on this. Shortly after our discussion, he was off to find materials to draw with. Remember he finds such comfort and pleasure in drawing his animals and Disney characters.

As the evening wore on, there was music and dancing inside while Julian settled at a table on the terrace of the restaurant with his pen and papers. A large glass window allowed me to stand at the bar talking with friends while keeping and eye on Julian who was a few feet away on the other side of the glass.

Throughout the evening, a number of the pre-adolescents, hopped up on cake, were running around the restaurant and chasing each other seemingly everywhere. They incurred the benign wrath of our friend Ranota's father who constantly warned the youngsters to slow down or face the consequences from him. He and I were chatting at one point, later in the night, when I noticed his eyes became fixed on a point behind me. With my back now to the glass, I couldn't share his view of the terrace.

"That's amazing," he said with an approving smile.

I turned and saw Julian, seated at a table drawing while surrounded by all those kids. Some were standing behind him watching every stroke of his pen while a couple others had secured paper and pen of their own and were copying what they saw Julian doing. It was as if he were some kind of child whisperer; they were all calm for the first time all evening. Mr. Thomas, Ranota's father, was beside himself.

"No one else could've done that but him."

"That's Julian," I replied.

"You've got a special boy there. He's going to do something in this world."

"Yes, sir, I know."

That night, we, in my mind, were celebrating the successes of two young men.

THE BEST INTEREST OF JULIAN

OCTOBER 20, 2011

Martina and I, filled with anxiety and unsure of what was about to happen, nervously discussed the weather, college football, the latest movies, new wines we wanted to try, anything to keep our mind off the uncertainty we both felt at that moment. We were seated in chairs at a witness table in the Durham (N.C.) Clerk of Court's courtroom awaiting the entrance of the clerk of court. Julian had recently, in late August, turned eighteen, and we were in the process of securing legal guardianship of him. This was something that had to be done for his best interest.

Although Julian has high-functioning autism, he still requires assistance to actually function on a daily basis. This has always been, and probably will always be, the case. Whether it's making sure he's dressed properly or helping him prepare a meal, he usually needs some level of guidance. While his level of independence will grow, we're not certain it will ever get to the point that would allow him to be fully self-sufficient. This point was underscored when a letter, addressed to him, arrived in the mail recently from the state Division of Motor Vehicles. The official and impersonal letter informed Julian that, due to his official diagnosis and our action to gain guardianship, he was deemed unfit to have a driver's license.

This seemed harsh to me, however, I fully understood it was proper procedure. I'd witnessed a bit of this recently when we began the legal guardianship process. Julian had to be, personally, served papers by a sheriff's deputy. The papers declared, in black and white, we were asserting that he was incompetent to care for himself and were seeking legal authority over him. The idea of a uniformed officer serving Julian papers set off all sorts of alarms in our heads. How would Julian interpret this? Would it upset him? Would he automatically think he'd done something wrong and was being punished?

We decided the best course of action was to explain to him that, since he was now eighteen, Martina and I had to take certain measures to ensure that we would be able to continue to take care of him the way we had always been doing. I think the key for Julian was that this meant his life would remain, as he had always known it to be, Martina and me there for him all the time. When presented to him in this manner, he was fine with everything.

So, on the day that he was to be served, I took him down to the municipal building. A sheriff's deputy, wearing a warm smile, handed Julian the papers. The irony of that action was Julian really had no serious comprehension of what was transpiring, beyond the basic level this was being done so Mom and Dad could continue taking care of him, Another step in the process was an in-home visit by a court-appointed guardian ad litem, who would assess whether or not we could provide a proper and nurturing environment for Julian and if this was indeed in his best interest.

When she visited, Julian had yet to come home from school. We sat in our dining room as Martina and I answered all manner of queries and talked extensively about Julian. We planned the visit so that we could begin our interview before Julian came home, but we wanted her to meet him, so the meeting was set up to allow her to still be there when he arrived. Martina and I were not quite sure how Julian would react to her actual presence and what questions she might have for him.

About forty-five minutes into the interview, Julian came bounding through the front door. His eyes immediately fixed on our visitor. He walked over, smiled and extended his hand to say hello as we introduced him and reminded him who she was and why she was there. He seemed a little uneasy and asked if he could go to his room and get one of his small animals. He clearly needed a bit of comfort that he could find only while clutching one of his toy figures. Upon his return, with a small hard plastic lion secured in his hand, she began to ask Julian a few questions about his life with us. He answered but continually looked to Martina and me for approval and reassurance that this was all going to be okay. He knew this was important and was about ensuring his well-being.

After another thirty minutes, she left. We talked with Julian about the visit. His only concerns were about how his life would be the next day and if this would impact on him being able to watch his Disney movies and play with his animals. When we assured him that his life would be the same, he asked to be excused so that he could go watch a movie. As he disappeared up the stairs, it occurred to me that Julian would be with us for a long time and that we would probably face some real challenges in helping him come to grips with life as an adult with autism. At that same moment, I felt incredibly fortunate to know and love my son.

When the clerk of court entered the hearing room, we stood until he instructed us to be seated. He was a pleasant man who clearly wanted to make us as comfortable as possible. The session was recorded; it was still only the three of us in the room. The guardian ad litem was unable to be present but had prepared a thorough report, which the clerk read earlier. He wanted to hear from us about Julian. When it was over, he declared that it was in the best interest of our son that we have legal guardianship over him. Things would continue to be as they were, just the way Julian wanted.

OF DISNEY AND CREATURES

J ulian's body was shaking with delight and his face was alight with total joy as he watched the commercial. It was for Disney World. Martina and I had called him into the room to see the new television spot for his favorite place in the world. The idea of an eighteen-year-old being so excited by a Disney commercial may seem odd at first, but this is Julian and ever since he was old enough to know what the Magic Castle represented, all things Disney have enthralled him.

In fact, just before rushing into the den to view the commercial, he was back in our home office, on the Internet, searching for information on and images of characters from Disney animated films. He possesses an expansive and deep reservoir of knowledge regarding Disney animated movies. There are the "Classics," such as Snow *White*, *Peter Pan*, *Lady and the Tramp*, to name a few. Then there is the more recent heading of "Renaissance" which features titles such as *The Lion King*, *Mulan* and *Aladdin*. Julian knows all the characters, major and minor, the actors who give voice to the stories, and the details of the respective soundtracks. This is his area of expertise.

As I've noted before, persons with autism often have specific areas of intense concentration and interest. For Julian, it's Disney and animals; more on the latter a little later. Not a day goes by that Julian doesn't engage us in some form of dialogue centered

Julian's desk in his bedroom
Courtesy of Dwayne Ballen

around the endlessly entertaining characters of these movies, be they heroes, villains or comic sidekicks. He knows them all and has an extensive DVD collection to support his interest. His favorite of all-time is *The Lion King*. Often he will call out to Martina and me, asking us to come up to his room, so that he might show us an array of Disney gold.

Usually, upon responding to his summons, we're greeted by his beaming countenance as he stands, proudly, over the DVD boxes that he has neatly arranged on his bed for his, or anyone else's, viewing pleasure. Meanwhile, one of the movies is playing on the monitor in his room while the soundtrack to another is blaring from his CD player. The conversation is always about his movies.

"Dad, I have a lot of Disney movies."

"A very impressive collection, son."

"Dad, who's your favorite Disney animated big cat character?"

"Who's yours?"

"Simba."

"Wow, mine too."

"What about the wickedest villain?"

"Maybe…Scar?"

"Yes! And Dr. Facilier (*The Princess and the Frog*)."

I thought I had made it through the quiz until Julian moved into, what seemed to me, the championship round of questioning.

"Dad, who would win if Sher Khan (*Jungle Book*) fought the Cheshire Cat (*Alice in Wonderland*)?"

"I would think Sher Khan, after all, he's a big tiger."

"But the Cheshire Cat has magical powers."

"Well, in that case, maybe the Cheshire Cat."

And so it can go on until I cry the proverbial uncle and admit to being no match for Julian in the world of Disney character information. This is Julian in full bliss. His love of Disney seems to only have grown stronger as he has gotten older. He is always inquiring about the possibility of adding another DVD or stuffed animal (representing a movie character) to his collection. Most recently we've been looking for a Dr. Facilier figurine. I'm not even sure such an item exists.

As for visiting the theme park in Orlando, well, it's like watching Julian enjoy his version of Nirvana. He's been four times. The first when he was not yet two years of age proudly left very little impression on him. At the time I was an anchor at The Golf Channel, which is based in Orlando. Martina, Julian and her mother were visiting me, so we decided to take him on his maiden Disney voyage. He spent most of the time in a stroller half asleep. The next three times, at ages ten, twelve and fifteen, were awesome.

I recall riding over to the Magic Kingdom in the ferry and seeing the sheer glee on his face as his body nearly came to convulsions,

Julian at Disney World in 2008
Courtesy of Dwayne Ballen

as we got closer. Standing at Disney World in the evenings and watching the fireworks show is a pure joy when you're in Julian's presence. We are planning another trip soon. I suspect this will never get old.

The other passion for Julian is the world of animals. It became evident, early in his young life, that he was drawn to animals. We took our first zoo trip with him when he was around two years of age and Julian was transported and transfixed. He would stare at the animals, in particular the lions, hardly moving, his eyes full of wonderment and joy. Pointing with his fingers and smiling. He could do this for extended periods of time; this world resonated with him.

As he grew older, animals became one of the dominate themes in his world. He has expressed interest in doing some sort of work with them when he's an adult: wildlife photographer, wildlife artist, etc. He even has told that he wants to live near the Serengeti wildlife reserve in eastern Africa, someday. Martina and I are constantly quizzed by Julian about animals, both real and mythical. He is his most animated when discussing them or Disney films.

One weekend evening, Julian asked me to sit with him as he scoured the Internet for information on animals. We found an animal cam on the National Geographic website. It is a permanent remote web cam posted at a watering hole at one of the wildlife reserves in Africa. We sat patiently, waiting, minutes, then an hour went by and nothing appeared at the watering hole. I excused myself, promising to return if he spotted any animals. However, Julian, undeterred by the lack of activity, was brimming with anticipation and excitement. He had music playing on a CD player, some of his small animal figures arrayed on the desk next to the computer, and a tall glass of lemonade in hand. He could sit for hours waiting and watching.

"Dad, come look at this!" I rushed in to see what Julian informed me was a kudu. An antelope that is indigenous to eastern and southern Africa. The animal, with legs slightly splayed, was quenching its thirst while continually raising its head to check for predators. It was nighttime at the sight of the web cam which made it seem a bit more eerie. I quickly learned from Julian that there are two species of kudu, lesser and greater. The males in the latter group have spectacular long spiral horns that can reach seventy-two inches in length. The one we were watching clearly belonged to this group. Julian was a fountain of information, and he was spouting. As eaters they are browsers, mostly dining on wooly plants and fruit. They possess powerful leaping ability, from a standing position an adult kudu can clear a fence five feet high. They can live, provided they avoid lions, hyenas, large reptiles, to twenty-three years of age. As he went on about this animal, I saw his sheer glee. He was rocking back and forth and pointing to the screen as he deluged me with facts about the kudu. This was my son in full flower.

His love of animals goes beyond simply watching them. He revels in the opportunity to spend any time around them doing anything. One summer, his "WELL Program" camp spent a day working at a horse farm. This allowed Julian the chance to spend time, up close and personal, with the horses. The pictures of him walking and brushing the horses are studies of someone at peace and contentment. No matter what task he was charged with, he carried it out with enthusiasm. Ms. Tiffane Land (WELL Program executive director) told me later that she'd never seen someone shovel horse manure with such care and apparent happiness; the entire time he had a wide grin crossing his face.

Martina and I are hopeful that somehow we will be able to help him incorporate his knowledge and love of animals into a vocation

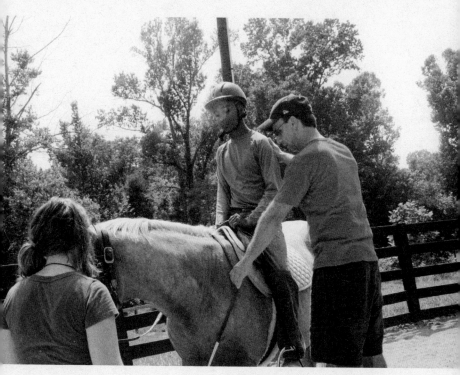

Julian rides a horse at WELL Program
Courtesy of the WELL Program

that is right for him. We also are considering ways to get him involved in animation, given his obvious talents and imaginative mind. Whatever his future work-related life entails, animals will always be a significant factor in Julian's world. Most recently, he has expressed a strong desire to become an animator for Disney. Now that, I think, would be perfect for all parties involved.

MAY 31, 2012-SEPTEMBER 10, 2012

JULIAN GOES TO CAMP

MAY 31, 2012

I had to resist the urge to turn the car around. We were on our way to take Julian to his first overnight camp. I wasn't completely comfortable with the idea of Julian being away from us like this. Understand, with the exception of visits to close relatives and friends and his time in the hospital, he had never spent a night away from home without either Martina or me with him. When his school would have end-of-year trips, one of us would always go along.

Martina and I had discussed this at length. It took quite a bit of convincing, on her part, before I acquiesced. I fully realize how odd this might seem to the average person; a father's anxiety over the thought of his eighteen-year-old son spending a weekend at camp. You must appreciate how much he has relied on us to help him with day-to-day maintenance matters that typical teenagers routinely perform as part of a personal daily regimen.

At night we're there to make sure he remembers things such as brushing his teeth and using the bathroom before going to bed. It is not uncommon for him to request that one of us come sit down with him, to talk, for a few minutes as he settles into bed. I lay out his clothes for him each evening. Julian gives little thought to what he wears. In fact, one recent morning, while I was preparing his breakfast, I looked up to see him descending the stairs wearing a big smile and two different shoes. I'd forgotten to put a pair out for him, so he reached into his closet and grabbed the first two he put his hands on.

Martina and I are acutely aware that Julian has to begin to gain a measure of relative self-reliance. We do want him to be able to live as independently as possible in the future. So, this weekend camp, which was specially designed for young adults with high-functioning autism, was really the right "first step." I had to let go a little.

The moment we turned onto the gravel driveway leading to the wonderfully bucolic setting that is home to the Autism Society of North Carolina's Camp Royall, near Chapel Hill, I began to feel a little better. It is the ideal place for Julian to attend camp. Lots of trees and trails, a pool, a lake and cabins to sleep in. If it housed a small zoo, it would be close to Nirvana for Julian.

As we helped him set up his room, we took great pains to make sure he was mindful of a few key points: remember to shower, take your medicine, these are the clothes you should wear at different times. His responses to this were, as always unfailingly polite and respectful, "Yes, sir," "Yes, ma'am," "I will, Dad," "Okay, Mom," "I promise, Dad." Once done with that task, we escorted him to the dining hall where there was an introductory spaghetti dinner planned for the campers. When we entered the hall, a number of them had already made their way through the serving line. One of the counselors greeted Julian and told him he could join in and get his food.

At that moment, she gave us a reassuring look that read, *He'll be fine. It will be fun!* Julian hugged us both and merrily headed off to his new adventure. I stood there and nearly followed behind him, but just as I started to move, Martina gently tugged my arm and said, "It's time for us to leave." It was actually a difficult moment for me; I started to tear up and quickly walked outside. I could hear Jared, our younger son, asking his mom, "Is Dad crying?" Yes, I was. Boy, this really was affecting me more than I anticipated.

That night we received an email from one of the counselors telling us that Julian was having a blast. The group had gone out to listen to some live music. Afterward, he took a flashlight and scoured the camp grounds in search of "night creatures." I so wanted to hear his voice, but my brilliantly intuitive and level-headed wife calmed me and suggested that we take satisfaction and comfort in the counselor's message. Of course she was right, but that didn't make it any easier for me.

His Saturday included swimming, hiking, a group dinner at a local restaurant and a telephone conversation with his parents. He sounded full of enjoyment. When we arrived Sunday morning to pick him up, he was out looking for "creatures" in the lake. When we walked into his room, his clothes were everywhere, and his toiletries and medicine were left in the community shower. I could tell he hadn't worn his clothes quite the way I'd laid out for him. None of that really mattered. A that moment we looked out the window and saw him walking back to the cabin, the picture of cheerfulness. It was obvious to me that our family had taken a significant first step with Julian.

As we left the camp, he was animated and flowing with stories about his weekend. I gazed at my son through the rearview mirror and realized, while going to camp is considered ordinary for most, it had been anything *but* for Julian, and his dad.

THE RELUCTANT BUT POLITE CELEBRITY

"Hi, Julian, I have autism also!" Those words were enthusiastically pouring out of a man in his early fifties. Out of respect for his privacy, we'll call him John (not his real name). He extended his hand and Julian smiled, said hello, quickly shook John's hand, then whirled forty-five degrees to his right to face his mom.

Martina immediately recognized the forced smile on his face and what it meant: Julian was not interested in having a dialogue with John about their shared membership in the community of persons with autism.

I had just delivered the morning's keynote address at the Autism Society of North Carolina's annual conference. I spoke about our life with Julian. As is always the case when I speak about this topic, my emotions ran the gamut from frustration and despair to joy, pride and unbridled hope. Julian was not present in the convention hall for my talk. Martina and I have decided that, right now, it may be a bit too much for him to sit and listen to what can be, at times, a very personal discussion of our family's ongoing journey. After the speech, I returned to our room to bring Julian to the convention hall for lunch and so that he could witness the rest of the day's program.

The talk was so well-received that many of the conference's attendees were anxious to meet Julian. As we entered the hall, many eyes were on him and people were greeting him and telling him how much they connected to his story. Though always a model of graciousness and respect in these settings, it was clear to Martina and me that Julian didn't want to enter into specific conversations about his autism. This is why he reacted in the manner that he did to "John."

One young lady wanted to take a picture with him—Julian's first fan! Well, if you don't count Martina or me. Another woman, who identified herself as a mother of a person with autism, simply wanted to hug him. I am mindful, as I write this blog, give more talks and move forward with the publishing of this book, that Julian will be drawn into the public sphere. I've talked to him about this and have always asked his permission—after all, it is his story—before proceeding with anything related to public communication about our family life and autism.

Before I began the blog, and later this book, I talked to him, at length, about both, well as much at length as Julian was willing to go. He thought it was a good idea to share our story and let others know about autism, but, to my knowledge, he's never read the blog. A number of times I've offered to read entries from the blog or book to him, then for the two of us to discuss the content. Always the response has been polite and clear. "Uh, that's okay, Dad. I'm fine."

However, a few weeks ago, I sat down at the computer in our home office and noticed among the minimized pages, at the bottom of the screen, was the home page for this blog. Jared was at basketball practice, Martina had yet to come home from work, and unless Tango, our rambunctious Glen of Imaal terrier, was surfing the web, that only left Julian and me. I didn't recall going to the site that day. Maybe it was left over from another day. Maybe not. Hm-m-m.

Recently, Jean Rheem, a young lady who's studied psychology and visual arts at Duke University and has volunteered with Julian's weekly social group for the last couple of years, produced a documentary short about the social group. When I asked Julian if he wanted to see it, his answer revealed some movement, albeit slow, on the idea of him discussing autism. "Not really. I'm okay. Well, maybe later. Will you watch it with me?"

We've now made a pact to sit and watch it as a family. We're just waiting on Julian to say he's ready, though Martina and I both are aware that we'll probably have to nudge him on the matter. Part of the reason for us wanting Julian to become more comfortable in discussing his autism is that we want him to be a confident and strong advocate for himself as an adult. To that end he has been asked to sit on the local advisory board of a non-profit First in Families as a self-advocate. We're not sure how vocal he will be, but this is definitely a move in the right direction. There is a board member who knows him and will serve as a point of comfort and encouragement for him.

One thing that was evident that day at the conference is that Julian can light up a room. He does enjoy talking to people and sharing his stories about animals and Disney. There have also been inquiries from Hollywood about potentially turning our story into a television show. When I asked Julian about possibly becoming a celebrity and helping to raise awareness about autism, he smiled and wondered if such status might get him a special trip to Disney World or the Serengeti wildlife reserve in Africa.

Julian, anything's possible.

THE MUSIC MAN

JUNE 11, 2012

I opened the CD case to find several of my favorites missing. Where was Marvin (Gaye)? Al (Green)? The Temptations? I was certain I'd put them all back in their cases. Where were those CDs? Maybe Martina had them in her car. No, she hadn't seen those particular ones. This was puzzling.

Later that evening, I was downstairs in the kitchen talking to Martina when we heard Al Green plaintively wailing he was "Tired of Being Alone." It was coming from Julian's room. I arrived at his door to find him listening to Green's greatest hits, watching Disney's *The Aristocats* on his television, and viewing *The Jungle Book* on an iPad. All this while proudly gazing down on his bed, arms akimbo, where he had arrayed his myriad Disney DVD box covers.

I've noted scenes like this before, where one can witness Julian's ability, or maybe need, to take in multiple auditory and visual streams at once. His face was the picture of bliss and contentment. I hesitated to interrupt his "flow," but I had to investigate the missing CDs. I found out that he did have all the ones I'd been looking for earlier that day. I can't say that I was totally surprised by my discovery.

Music has been a major component in Julian's life. When he

was younger, and not too verbal, music could always get him going. He'd clap his hands and attempt to sing along. As he got older, he always wanted his portable CD player with him. It was interesting to watch us pile into the car, to go anywhere. The market, the park, the mall. The destination didn't matter; he would haul that player and about ten CDs around, along with his stuffed animals. Boy, was the iPod a welcome innovation in our house.

I think, amateur psychiatrist that I am, the music has served to help Julian find a calming place when he might otherwise be overwhelmed with the world and its demands. Every night, before he goes to bed, he is listening to music. His preference has always been R&B, Disney soundtracks and classic soul. The latter came from hearing something Martina and I were playing for our own enjoyment.

The dialogue usually goes as follows.

"Dad, who's that?"

"Earth, Wind and Fire."

"When was that made?"

"When I was a kid."

"I think I like it! May I listen to it?"

Of course we always hand over the CD, never to see it again—well, maybe in passing while in Julian's room. Remember when someone with autism latches on to something, they usually can't let go. Martina and I are well aware of this fact, so whenever he inquires about one of our CDs, we know it's good-bye. There is a certain look she gives me when this occurs. It's one that suggests it was fun, having the CD in question, while it lasted. We joke that Julian's room is a graveyard for CDs. It probably will not surprise you to know that we regard this as a very small price to pay, for Julian to have something that brings him such comfort.

Sometimes, it even comes in the form of "out of season" musical fare. It is not uncommon, in the spring or dead of summer, to hear holiday music spreading its cheer from Julian's room. As Martina will attest to, one of her favorites, Vanessa Williams' outstanding Christmas CD, has been heard on the Fourth of July in our house. It works for Julian and that's what counts.

At the time of this writing, I took a moment and walked to the bottom of the stairs and could hear Marvin Gaye's "Can I Get a Witness" coming from his room. It brought a smile to my face. A few minutes later, when I had returned to my writing in our home office, Julian dropped in to visit. I had Smokey Robinson and his greatest hits CD playing in the background. "The Tears of a Clown" was reaching its end when I recognized that look of excited discovery on Julian's face.

"Hey, Dad, who's that?"

Uh-oh. Nice knowing you, Smokey.

Julian's animal drawing in the sand on the beach in August 2008
Courtesy of Dwayne Ballen

DAD, HOW WAS YOUR DAY?

JUNE 18, 2012

I was sitting down reading during late afternoon when Julian walked up and asked, "So Dad, how was your day?" This was mildly startling. Julian expressing interest in how things were going for me. It's not that he doesn't care, I know he does. It's the fact that persons with autism have such a difficult time with matters such as feeling empathy or the concerns of others.

One of the reasons is their inability to pick up on social cues: reading facial expressions, correctly picking up on body language, knowing when someone is joking or being sarcastic; the list goes on and on. Probably even more of a factor is an intense, inwardly focused worldview evinced by the vast majority of persons with autism. If it's not about their respective interests, then it just doesn't resonate as much.

Martina and I have attempted to introduce the concept, thinking about others' interests and feelings, into Julian's world, with limited progress, but progress nonetheless. Again, it's not that he doesn't feel; it's that he has a degree of social communication deficit, which makes it more difficult for him to access those feelings as easily as neurotypical persons can.

On Father's Day, Julian wanted to go to our community pool. He loves the water, and we told him that we'd probably go over in the early evening when the sun was down and it was cooler. After an enjoyable dinner with the boys, Martina and I sat on our back deck with a nice bottle of wine and Sinatra playing in the background. It was a pleasant and almost blissful setting. We decided we would delay the pool visit by one day. Now, to tell Julian.

When we told him, the initial reaction was expected. His face slightly contorted, he was confused, a bit upset. We promised he could go to the pool. Martina took his hand, and in a very calm and reassuring tone, told him he would go the next day. She then looked at me and reminded Julian that it was Father's Day.

"Your dad is really enjoying sitting here on the deck and relaxing. Since it's Father's Day, don't you think it would be nice to let him continue doing just that?"

Julian looked at me, frowned, and then smiled and said, "Okay, of course. I'm sorry, Dad." It was clear that his emotions were swinging back and forth. He wanted to understand, but he was unhappy that he wouldn't be going to the pool. He went into the house, only to return moments later, still searching for a comfortable resolution in his mind. He pronounced, "I'm okay. I don't have to go." However, his body language said something else. He was clearly anxious and obviously interested in still trying to negotiate that trip to the pool. I was ready to give in and take him, but we'd decided this would be a good opportunity to try to get him to really consider someone else's feelings.

After several trips in and out of the house, with us continually reminding him that today was for dad, he finally decided he needed to go for a walk. I felt sorry for him, but I knew we needed to try this; he is going to be in a society where others may not always be interested in "his world" or his desires. We know that it's working because of the aforementioned inquiry about how my day was going. In fact, this has occurred a number of times recently.

"Dad, how are you doing today?" "Dad, are you happy today?" It is quite touching to look at his face as he makes such earnest efforts to think of someone else.

As for our little "exercise" regarding the pool, when he returned from his walk, he was much calmer and smiling, genuinely. I was inside the house as he entered the kitchen. We talked a bit more about considering the "wants" of other people. It ended with him, unprompted, telling me he hoped I'd had a good Father's Day. I told him it had been good.

When he started to walk off, then quickly turned around to engulf me in a hug, it became a great day.

A TOUGH DAY

JUNE 28, 2012

Julian's face was tense and his hands were shaking as he began to speak. "Dad! I don't know what to do!" He was having a meltdown. I had seen this before, more than a few times. When he was younger this was, unfortunately, a regular occurrence. These incidents have become fewer and far between, but when they do happen, the intensity and frustration levels are very high. So here was my eighteen-year-old son, frankly, "losing it" and there was little I could do, despite my efforts, to make him feel better.

It began that morning as Martina was leaving for work. Julian began repeating, with increasing intensity, a couple of statements and questions.

"Mom, my life is going to be good."

"I know, honey, it will be fabulous!"

"You know that."

"I'm positive!" She was doing her best to be encouraging and upbeat.

"You know that!" Julian, inexplicably, was beginning to get agitated.

"Yes, honey."

This exchange continued for a few more repetitions with Julian's anxiety level increasing. Despite her, and later my, assurances, nothing could calm Julian. We are well aware that he is concerned about his future; he has one more year of high school. There are family friends his age already in college. Jared, our younger son, is participating in SAT preparatory programs. We have numerous discussions with Jared, a rising junior, about potential colleges and what it will take to be ready. We have also talked with Julian about this subject.

We have always told him that he will continue his education after high school. But on this day, nothing that we said, in the way of encouragement or support, mattered. I can't tell you that there was a specific trigger for this because, to our knowledge, there wasn't. That is the nature of autism meltdowns. Your child can go from calm to nearly raging in an instant, with no reason or forewarning. After Martina left the house, it was just the two of us. Jared was away at basketball camp.

Persons who care for someone with autism are probably very familiar with how the rest of the day unfolded. Julian had taken off on an emotional rocket: at times hitting himself in the head, throwing himself on the floor, making unprovoked aggressive moves toward me and making high-volume pronouncements that indicated he wished harm to me and Martina. It is not an easy thing to witness your child this way.

I knew full well he really didn't mean any of the things he was saying or doing, but it was happening. I kept my voice at a modulated level and tried to keep him engaged. What was wrong? Why would you say that? You know we love you and don't want you to hurt yourself. You have such a bright future. You are going to have a great life. This is not the proper way to behave. No matter what words came out of my mouth, he was not satisfied. In his mind, things simply were not right at the moment. So

I had to sit there and make sure my son did nothing drastic as we rode out this emotional storm together.

When Julian gets like this, he can say some very hurtful things.

"Dad, I hate you! I hope the Dalmatians attack you!"

Suddenly catching himself, he will quickly change tones and tell me he's sorry, but two minutes later, he's saying something mean again. This can go on for a couple of hours. A brief humorous aside. Julian's mention of the Dalmatians is a reference to Disney's animated classic, *101 Dalmatians*. Yes, even in a state such as he was in, his beloved Disney animated films are never far from his mind.

Julian's development and determination, along with the care of an exceptional therapist, have helped to dramatically reduce these episodes. They have, thankfully, become fewer and very far between. Afterward, when he has settled down, we have a lengthy discussion about what happened. It is rare that he can fully explain what upset him. He is always contrite and very embarrassed at this point. He tells us he knows full well how much we love him and how much he loves us. We make it clear that he has hurt our feelings and his behavior is not acceptable. We even let him help decide on proper punishment.

It is interesting that these outbursts almost never take place outside the home. Martina likes to say that he saves it for us because we're special. At the end of the day, he and I sat together in his room. It was obvious how much his actions bothered him.

"Dad, I'm sorry. I shouldn't do those things."

"You're right, you shouldn't. Your mother and I don't deserve that kind of treatment."

"I really love you and Mom...and Jared."

"We love you, too, son."

Despite incidents such as this one, which are now infrequent, we feel very fortunate to receive the many displays of love and affection that Julian showers us with on a daily basis. As I've shared with you before, that is not common in the world of autism.

Difficult? Tough? Sure, on occasion, it can be hellish. But you know what? He's still one of the sweetest, considerate and most loving people you will ever meet. He's our Julian.

THE POOL BOYS

JULY 16, 2012

Julian wanted to go to our community pool; in fact, he'd already donned his swim trunks and flip-flops and located his goggles. The last of that trio being nearly essential for his enjoyment in the water. We had, earlier in the day, promised him he could go, so he was just waiting for Martina and me to gather ourselves so that we could all go, Jared included. It is a rare summer day that Julian doesn't want to go for a swim. He has always loved the water. Everything about being in close proximity to a pool, ocean, lake, any form of water, even a Jacuzzi or large tub, brings him joy.

I recall a vacation trip to a coastal resort that really drove home this point. We'd spent the entire day, emphasis on the word *entire*, on the beach. That evening, after dinner, Julian settled in on the balcony of our oceanfront condo and took in the waves, sound and wind for hours. He was content to simply sit there, watching and listening well into the night. Some experts believe that the affinity persons with autism have for the water has to do with the sensory pleasure derived from the total immersion in something that doesn't push back. Others posit that the dramatic decrease in noise, while underwater, is especially soothing to them. In or out of the water, Julian is happy as long as he's near it.

With that in mind, you can understand how anxious Julian was for us to get going. At that moment, I decided to try something different. "Why don't you and Jared go? Mom and I will stay here." This caught both boys off-guard. Previously, a trip to the pool always included either Martina or me, most times the both of us. But, at eighteen, we must allow Julian more opportunities to take small steps toward independence. Plus, we thought it would be good for both our sons.

Jared, who is now sixteen, has lived with Julian's autism for nearly all his life. While he has done a good job of trying to understand, and adapt to, his brother's differences, it has not been easy for him. Sometimes they argue and fight. While not uncommon among siblings, especially teenage boys, these disagreements occasionally lay bare the frustration Jared feels, at times, with Julian. One particular instance, after hearing some very loud bumping and shouting, I found myself upstairs separating the two.

I sent Julian to his room, then addressed Jared. Sometimes it can be hard to trace the origin of the argument when Julian is involved. Such was the case that evening. I reminded Jared of the myriad conversations we'd had about the high tolerance and patience levels required, on our part, when Julian is upset. At that point, I went on to explain, it didn't matter so much with whom the fault lay as it did how Jared handled the situation.

This is the part of the equation that would seem unfair to Jared, but it goes to the nature of him being the brother of someone with autism. The burden of resolution falls more on him than Julian. Not the easiest concept for a typical sixteen-year-old to accept.

It's not that Julian gets a free pass. We make sure that he fully understands the consequences of his actions and realizes he will be held accountable. It's just that, in the heat of the moment, diffusing a confrontational situation is more likely to come from

Julian enjoys the ocean in August 2008
Courtesy of Dwayne Ballen

the person without autism. As Jared and I talked about this, his eyes welled up and he released.

"Dad, why does he act like that? Sometimes I think he hurts our family. He ruins everything. He makes me so mad sometimes. This just isn't fair." I listened and allowed him to get it all out. Then, with my arm around him, I asked him to put himself in Julian's place. Did he really think his brother's true intent was to cause problems for the family? Could he conceive of living life in a world that is not designed with someone like you in mind? What if he was eighteen and had never been able to even approach a girl and have a sustained conversation with her?

Our discussion went on for about thirty more minutes. I offered no easy answers but assured Jared that the strongest bond our family has is our love for each other and that was unbreakable, no matter what disagreements arose. As I left his room and descended the stairs, I heard him walk into Julian's room and apologize. Interestingly, Julian reciprocated.

So, my decision to send them off together to the pool was a way of forcing them to talk a little more and continue to find ways to connect with each other. About an hour-and-a-half later, I looked out the front window to see them walking back. Laughing, and apparently at ease with one another. Brothers. Later, when I asked Jared how it went, he said well.

"Dad, we actually had a cool conversation. We talked about Disney animation and girls. It was really nice. I was kinda surprised."

"That's nice, glad the two of you could hang out and enjoy each other, without us around. All it took was a little effort."

"He really is special. I want you to know I'll always be there for him."

"I know."

JULIAN, THE VOLUNTEER

AUGUST 22, 2012

"You have your lunch?"

"Yes, sir."

"You know where to go?"

"Uh-h, yes, sir."

"I'm very proud of you."

"Thank you, Dad!"

With that exchange concluded, Julian was out of the car and on his way into the home of our local arts council to begin a few days of volunteer work for a children's art camp. As I watched him disappear into the building, I felt pangs of anxiousness. I admit to having some separation anxiety when it comes to Julian, and rushes of joy. He was doing something for someone else and was excited about it.

When Martina and I first discussed the idea of Julian doing volunteer work, it was a matter of finding a situation where he wouldn't be overwhelmed but would have the opportunity to contribute in his own way, a setting that he would feel comfortable in. It had to be somewhere that would allow for his autism and recognize that he needed specific instruction. This turned out to be perfect.

The camp director and I agreed that it would probably be best

Julian volunteers with children at WELL Program
Courtesy of the WELL Program

if Julian worked a half-day. We weren't sure how he would handle a full day. This was a first for him. When I arrived to pick him up, I found my way to one of the large meeting halls where the campers were having lunch. Kindergartners were everywhere. It was noisy and animated. I didn't see Julian. He was in the restroom but immediately spotted the camp director.

She approached me, face beaming and clasping her hands together. "He's been awesome! We'd love to have him stay for the full day." Turns out, working with small kids fit Julian just fine. She informed me that his demeanor was calm and patient with them. His job was to help them with various art projects. During breaks, he would enthrall the youngsters with his drawings. He took requests from them, the most popular being Mickey Mouse and the Disney princesses. Boy, talk about being in his wheelhouse. I was quite happy to leave and return later so that he could complete a full day.

When I finally did return to pick him up, I found him in the office sitting with a little boy who was hanging on to Julian's every word. He was telling the boy about cryptids, mythological creatures such as the Yeti or the Chupacabra. At that very moment, I saw just how right this was for Julian. Though he is nearly nineteen years of age, socially, he's closer to that kindergarten-aged child than to an adult. He's able to converse with children on a level that is easy for him. They find his interest fascinating. There is a sweet innocence that is apparent when watching him with children.

The director couldn't stop talking about how great he was with them. In fact, when his week was done, she asked if it would be possible to have him involved with more of their camps for kids. Julian thought it was a great idea and I was overjoyed for him. He truly was happy because he'd helped someone else. What a milestone.

On our way home, I asked him what it was like working with all those kids. "It was fun, I like it. It's kind of like working with animals." Now understand, that's the highest compliment Julian could pay those children because he loves animals and thinks any time with them is awesome. So, from Julian's perspective, equating a group of kindergartners with animals is a very good thing.

The weekend following his week of camp work, Julian volunteered to help man a booth for our local First in Families chapter, a group that assists families and persons with autism. It was part of a community outreach day sponsored by the local ARC. As was the case with the camp, this was something new for him. In this particular instance, he would have to talk about autism as he explained the services provided by FIF to those visiting the booth.

Given his reluctance to engage in prolonged discussion about his autism, Martina and I weren't sure how he would handle this, but we reminded him that this was more about the assistance FIF provides to people who really need it and that he was doing a very good thing. We also pointed out that by doing this, he was showing everyone that autism didn't stop him from doing productive things. And once again, this was an example of him thinking of others as opposed to himself. When we arrived at the park where the event was held, Wanda Brown, the chapter director, was there waiting for him and eager to participate.

Martina and I decided to make ourselves scarce, lest he fixate on us being around and not fully engage in the task at hand. We found a place where he couldn't see us, but we could watch him.

I can't tell you how proud we were to watch him shake hands and carefully read from the pamphlet as he explained about FIF to the constant stream of visitors. It was a really good day for Julian. As we were leaving, Julian had already gone to the car, and a lady stopped me.

"Excuse me, was that your son at the First in Families booth?"

"Yes, his name is Julian."

"Well, I want you to know that he was so sweet and considerate that I decided to participate and contribute to First in Families. All because he was so nice and took time to read every word of that flyer so that I understood what they were about. He's such a special young man."

Yeah, I get that a lot.

HEY NINETEEN, IT'S JULIAN

SEPTEMBER 10, 2012

As I rose one recent morning, wiped the sleep from my eyes and opened the door to our bedroom, I was greeted by Julian, already up and ready for the day, wearing a big grin with his arms open for an embrace. "It's my birthday!" Yes it was (his nineteenth), so I gave him a big hug and a kiss. I knew what he wanted to do for the day, after school of course, but I decided to ask anyway. He wanted to go through this again; it was written all over his face.

"So, what do you think we're going to do today?"

"I want to get a puffin (a stuffed toy animal that is a relative of the penguin) and another sea creature, go to Chinese 35, and will you watch a Disney movie with me?"

"Of course, anything else?"

"Do I have any cards?"

"Wait and see. First, you do have school."

What caught me off-guard about that exchange was Julian's query referencing the birthday card. We've always had cards for him on his birthday but, frankly, Martina and I never thought they registered to him, only the gifts. I assumed that given his fixation on things such as stuffed toy animals and Disney movies that he paid little attention to the cards we got him.

We are quick to presume the only things that resonate with Julian are those which fall under the categories of his special interests. That his world is so insular, very little else gets in beyond his "favorites." Well, that's not really the case. He takes in much more than we realize. This is probably true of most persons with autism. Though they may not necessarily communicate it to those of us who care for them, you might be surprised to find out exactly what they take note of in the external world.

Moment of embarrassing truth here, Martina and I actually had dropped the proverbial ball regarding his birthday card. Each of us thought the other had picked one up. The night before, when we discovered our oversight, we comforted each other with the thought that as long as Julian had his new animals, a meal at his favorite Chinese restaurant and got to watch a Disney animated movie, he would be fine. Therefore, when asked by him, we both made it seem that the plan was for the card to be revealed along with his gifts during his birthday dinner.

It is amazing to think that he is now nineteen and beginning his senior year of high school. We have traveled such a long way in that period of time with our eldest son. He has shown remarkable resilience and a steely will to experience a full life, traits that I wish all of us could command. The road ahead is uncertain and causes me now a small amount of anxiety, but I draw my strength from Julian. He is quick to say to me, "Dad, I will have a great life and be successful." Partly, he offers this so that I will provide reaffirmation. But another part is a deeply held belief in himself.

At dinner that evening, we presented him with cards, Jared read a touching note he'd written about what his big brother meant to him, and of course, he received his stuffed animals. It was interesting to watch the reactions of the other diners as this handsome nineteen-year-old erupted in pure glee upon the sight of those toy animals. When I scanned them, the other patrons of the restaurant, what I saw were smiles accompanied with looks of approval and a measure of instant understanding. Julian doesn't even realize how he is helping to make the world more accepting of thousands like him, simply by being himself.

That night, prior to turning in for the evening, I stood in the doorway of his room and watched him sleep. Positioned on the edge of his bed (to make room for all the stuffed animals he shares it with), arms around a large stuffed lion and the puffin in his hand, with the hint of a smile on his face, he was off somewhere in his dreams. My gaze traveled just beyond his resting body to his desk where he had carefully placed both cards we'd given him.

It was a very good birthday, for all of us.

Ballen family: (from left) Jared, Martina, Julian and Dwayne, 2011
Courtesy of Dwayne Ballen

HAVE YOU EVER THOUGHT, WHAT IF?

"Mr. Ballen, have you ever had thoughts of bitterness? Wondering why this happened to your son, your family?" The question caught me somewhat off-guard. It came from an audience member at a recent speaking engagement. The simple answer is no. Our family is part of a steadily growing community affected by autism. I imagine most would agree that you have little time for toxic emotions such as bitterness. You concentrate so much on your child and building a support system that will provide them with the best chance for a successful, on their terms, life that there is scant room for little else that doesn't aid that mission.

I have, however, from time to time, considered the "what ifs." What if Julian's autism was more severe? What if Jared also had autism? That latter question is something that a number of families we know have dealt with, having multiple children on the spectrum. Some of the most anxious moments Martina and I experienced in Jared's young life occurred while we monitored his early development searching for the telling signs: slow verbal progress, parallel playing, repetitive behavior, etc.

We were well aware that the chances of Jared having autism were increased because of what experts refer to as genetic suscepti-bility. Fortunately, what could have been an especially stressful period didn't last too long as Jared quickly evinced signs of typical development. Martina and I actually feel that Jared's hyper social personality may have helped Julian. As toddlers it was common to see Jared pulling and tugging at Julian in an effort to engage him in play. Julian, who usually wanted no part of it, would eventually have to give his sibling some attention. Though they are both now teenagers, this formula still plays itself out in our household. Jared will use most any method of inducement to get a reaction from Julian. Sometimes it is a kind word about Julian's artwork or a question about a Disney movie. Sometimes it's in the form of a mild taunt or tease, the type of things that usually occur between most siblings. Martina and I look at each other and are thankful that, at least, they're communicating.

As for the former point, I considered, while reflecting on the question, what if Julian's autism was more severe? Seventy-five to 80 percent of persons with autism have severe mental challenges. Knowing this, Martina and I feel, most days, that we are among the more fortunate in the autism community. We have lively discussions with our son. He is quite able and willing to display affection. Life with him has its real challenges, but it also is fun.

Bitterness? No. Anxiety? Trepidation? Frustration? Concern for his future? All, yes. Recently, Julian has been asking a lot about how we think his future will play out. Will he have a girl-friend/wife? What will she look like? Will she be as pretty as Mom? What type of work will he do? Will he go to college? Will he be happy? How does one answer those questions? We choose to be encouraging and reaffirming with a tinge a reality.

For instance, on the matter of college, we tell him it is certainly possible, we would like that for him and will do everything to ensure that he continues his education after high school. We inform him it may be difficult and he has to be willing to work hard. Now a junior, Julian has one more year of high left so he, naturally, wants to know what's next. We (Martina, Julian and me) recently paid a visit to the University of North Carolina-Greensboro to learn more about its "Beyond Academics" program.

It is specifically designed for persons with developmental disabilities. One of the few of its kind in the entire country, the program provides various levels of support for students but allows them to go to college and be immersed in campus life like all other students. Participants work toward a four-year certificate.

When we visited, Julian was greeted by a young man who had been in the summer "WELL Program" with him. Remington was completing his freshman year and spoke to the group about how much he was enjoying life as a college student. His roommate was another young man Julian knew from the WELL Program. We'd already visited with Remington's parents about Julian rooming with them if he got into the program.

As we toured the small and intimate campus, Martina and I agreed that there was a sense of security that we found comforting. Though I must confess, I'm still an emotional ocean away from coming to terms with Julian away from us, in college. The visit went well and the program director indicated it would be a pleasure to have Julian on campus. We later were informed by his teachers that, upon his return from the visit, he was brimming with excitement about his college visit and attending UNC-G.

As to the question of a girlfriend? Recently, I was chatting with Julian in his bedroom prior to his turning in for the night and the topic, brought up by him, girls.

"Dad, what will my girlfriend be like?"

"I'm sure she will be very nice and share your interests."

"I want her to look like Mom."

"Your mother is quite beautiful, that would be nice."

"Do you think there's a girl out there for me?"

"I really do, but you have to give it time and know that you may have a few disappoints, as most men do with women, before you find the right one."

"Do girls think I'm handsome?"

"Of that I am sure."

"I don't have to rush, do I?"

"No, you don't."

Conversations like that find me fighting back tears. I know full well Julian has myriad social hurdles to overcome if he is to find the right companion. He's now eighteen and nearing the end of his junior year in high school. The inquiries about girls are coming at me with more frequency. He asks questions that a neurotypical person wouldn't ask. What color will her hair be? What will she look like? What will her name be? These missives are fired at me a couple of times a week. It may seem odd to you, but for Julian, it's part of his process. My answers are really questions back to him. What do you think is a nice hair color? What names do you like? This allows him talk through the idea of a girlfriend. These are the things he considers essential; remember Julian doesn't really grasp what being in a relationship, like that, would require.

So I engage him on this in the hope that we'll eventually begin to help him understand what it takes to really "have a girlfriend." There is an innocence about him that could easily lead to someone taking advantage of him and/or breaking his heart. This causes me anxiety but not bitterness. Because I truly do believe that out there, somewhere, is a young lady for my wonderful son.

My final thought on the question, I fielded during my talk, is that we've spent so much time learning, laughing and loving with Julian that bitterness has simply never been a part of the equation. Julian's presence has been a gift to us; one that continually gives so much more than it takes. Our lives would be less than, without him.

HIGH SCHOOL, THEN WHAT?

Getting Julian through school has been no small feat. Seared into my mind are the memories of a meeting with a school principal, as Julian was nearing the end of middle school. The man, as politely as possible, made it very clear that his school was not the place for Julian and that they felt they'd done all they could, or would do, for Julian. We had equally distressing meetings, during his first couple of years of high school, with administrators and support staff. None of them really seemed to know what to do with our son. Or how to really help him.

We did find one champion in the form of a (then) assistant principal, Ms. Willa Sample. One of those "forces of nature" you hear about, she was determined that Julian be given every opportunity to find a pathway to success. With the growing number of persons with autism entering our school systems, we need more Willa Samples. Currently, our primary educational system, as structured, is ill-equipped to meet the needs of this growing population.

The resolution to Julian's high school experience came to us as a residual of his mental breakdown. It was only after his hospitalization and the realization that full-time attendance at his chosen public high school wasn't going to work out, did we find out about the school he settled into for completion of high school. It's a specialized, little-publicized, school for children who are recovering from such mental setbacks as Julian endured.

Turns out that the Lakeview Therapeutic Learning Center, that's the official name, is perfect for Julian. Class sizes are about six kids to a room and the entire student body isn't more than twenty-five. The staff is amazing, attentive and patient. Learning is built around each child's strengths and interests. It has been wonderful to watch Julian flower at the school. One teacher recently confided to Martina and me that when Julian first arrived, barely speaking, unwilling to hold a pencil, in a near toddler state that he declared to the others, "There's nothing we can do for this child."

He was, happily, proven wrong as Julian, aided by their nurturing and patience, emerged from his shell. That same teacher now counts Julian as one of the school's minor marvels. Julian has even been asked to give prospective students and parents tours of the facility. As we come toward the end of his high school years, he is a solid "B" student with confidence and pride in his academic achievement.

The fact remains that had it not been for his illness, we may never have found the proper "educational home" for Julian. What would've happened? There are many families in this country struggling with this issue right now. Finding a place for their child with autism in a school system that simply isn't prepared for them. These children are much too bright and promising to be placed in a special needs class and, for all intents and purposes, forgotten about, rarely getting the opportunity to showcase their ability to thrive and grow.

Julian is especially proud that he will graduate from high school. We've recently ordered his cap and gown. There was a time, in the not too distant past, that Martina and I couldn't conceive of Julian getting to this point. So, that loud revelry you hear in late spring of 2013 will be the party we have for his graduation. Julian will have a well-deserved and hard-earned blowout!

As for college we've applied to the "Beyond Academics" program at the University of North Carolina-Greensboro. It is a non-degree program for persons with developmental disabilities. It allows for the student to have the full college experience without the pressure of having to complete a degree program. However, if the student so desires and has the ability, nothing prevents them from entering a degree program while still accessing the services provided by BA.

Watching his joy as we made a campus visit, I was so happy for my son. Jared, at this point, had already visited Harvard, Columbia, Morehouse, North Carolina and Georgia Tech, to name a few. Julian, very aware of this fact, would often query Martina and me about where he would attend college. It provided for some heart-wrenching moments as we assured him that he would continue his education beyond high school. Growing up on the campus of the University of North Carolina, he always expected to attend UNC.

Not understanding how difficult it is to be accepted into a school with Carolina's academic standards, Julian would tell anyone who asked that he would be a student at Chapel Hill. The emergence of the BA program at UNC-G has provided us with a viable and real possibility. One of the most endearing, however small, moments occurred as we were leaving the closing seminar during our visit to UNC-G. The director of Beyond Academics walked up to Julian, shook his hand, called Julian by name and told him how much UNC-G wanted him as a student. I can't adequately put into words how powerful and moving that was to me. Julian's face was aglow with the pride of knowing he was wanted, by a college. So now, he tells anyone who inquires that he will attend UNC-G.

The BA program provides, for a fee, specially trained personnel to provide individual assistance, at whatever level is necessary, for each student. As I noted earlier, he has two friends already enrolled in the program. They are excited about having Julian join them, and the prospect of him becoming their roommate. How prepared are we for this major transition in his life? Well, let's simply acknowledge that we have more preparation ahead.

I recognize that I will have no small amount of separation anxiety when the time comes. Julian and I have become very close over the years and share a bond that is, by the account of anyone who knows us, incredibly strong. Martina has joked that we may as well enroll me in the program; otherwise, I'll be a basket case, worrying about Julian. The good thing is that he has something to look forward to and for that, we are thankful.

Beyond school, Julian has expressed a definite desire to be an animator for Disney. I can think of no better match. His imagination is boundless, his gifts as an artist are obvious, and his love, specifically for Disney animation, is unquestionable. So don't be surprised if one day in the future, as you're watching the credits roll on the latest Disney animated film, the name of Julian Ballen appears as an animator.

That would truly be awesome.

FATHERS OF SONS

Tears were streaming down her face as she approached me. "I wish my husband had been here. I...may I hug you?" We embraced, and the lady I'd just met took a few minutes to tell me how difficult things had become in their household. Her husband simply was refusing to deal with the realities of having a son with autism. I had just finished giving a talk at a fundraiser for iCan House, a non-profit that assists persons with social skills difficulties, such as those normally associated with autism.

As the woman spoke to me, it was clearly evident how emotional and taxing their life had become. Her husband would not accept their adolescent son's autism. She explained that he didn't recognize that their son wasn't acting in a certain manner to be contrarian. Instead, he initially insisted on disciplining the child as though he were neurotypical. In other words, he was determined to "straighten the boy out." Eventually, the father distanced himself from the son and the mom has been left alone to do the heavy lifting.

I had a connected conversation with some women attending an event in Las Vegas in the fall of 2012. I was asked to speak at the Els for Autism foundation's annual gathering. Founded by professional golfer Ernie Els and his wife, Liezl, the charity, inspired by the Els' son, Ben, who has autism, has set a goal of raising $30 million to build an autism Center for Excellence in Jupiter, Florida.

Following my speech, I visited with two women who were young mothers of, relatively, recently diagnosed sons on the autism spectrum. Both expressed frustration with the struggles their husbands were having in connecting with their sons. It was clear, from the moms, that these men loved their sons. It just wasn't what they expected when they anticipated having a son.

Most of the men I know, personally, who have sons with autism are involved and exceptional fathers. But, as I have learned, there is a significant segment of fathers who do not handle autism, especially in their sons, very well. If you consider the weighty expectations our society places on what it means to "be a man," then maybe it shouldn't surprise anyone to hear stories of men who have problems relating to a son who's different. For most men, that son is their legacy; they and their name may one day be judged by the deeds of that progeny. This boy is charged with carrying on the family's dignity and honor.

Having recognized, and allowed for, this societal expectancy, I have this thought to share with those troubled dads: "It's not about you!" It is about that young boy who, despite behavior that you may not understand and that might (at times) defy conventional norms, really needs you in his life, not on the periphery but actively involved, day to day. To abandon your station and leave the daunting task of raising a son with autism to his mother is not only wrong but, frankly, it's cowardly and will shortchange you.

I speak of this from experience. When Julian was first diagnosed (at age four), I had to go through periods of adjustment and acceptance. At first I wanted to "make him understand" what was going to be proper conduct and what wasn't. Any son of mine would comport himself in a manner that reflected positively on our family and me. Note the latter part of that statement, emphasis on the word "me." I was concerned about what it would say about me, as a man, if my son were perceived as "different." Autism was not in my playbook for the well-planned life of achievement I had laid out for my son. I'm certain there are fathers out there right now feeling this way. Again, it's not about you!

As almost always has been the case, in major transformative stages of my adult life, Martina played a lead role in getting me to where I needed to be, emotionally and logically. During especially hard times, she would remind me Julian was not intentionally acting out; his lack of conforming to my rules was not a direct challenge to my authority. He had autism, it was different. I had to accept this. I had to learn, it wasn't about me!

I recall one incident when he was about five, Julian had a major meltdown: tearing his room up, ripping things off of the wall, breaking his own toys, being extremely disruptive. This had become regular theater in our house. I was done, it was going to stop. I would see to that. I was ready to really take matters "into my on hands." Martina interceded, calmed and sat me down, then presented me with a small stack of literature about autism. It wasn't the first time she'd suggested that I learn more about what we were dealing with, but it was the first time that I really listened to her. She knew that I'd resisted educating myself, in detail, about autism. This particular time she was resolute and unyielding, "You must read some of this and really think about things." Her words were clear and to the point. I still had yet to realize it wasn't about me!

I heeded her advice: actually that word suggests a choice to take it, or not. Hers was not a request; I had to wake up to the realities of our life with Julian. I did, and as I came to terms with my son's autism, it opened up a level of connection whit him that I'd previously thought impossible. Over time we came to rely on each other. He would let me know what he needed, how he was feeling and I always assured him that I was proud of him, loved him without conditions and would always be there for him. Guess what? I finally understood it wasn't about me.

To those fathers feeling disconnected and thinking this isn't what you signed up for when you thought of fatherhood, may I suggest you consider your child. Imagine what his world is like. He may not ever say it, he may not be capable of expressing it, but he wants and needs your guidance. I promise you it is not your son's intent to make you appear less of a man because of his differences. As for the "looks" you'll receive in public, especially as he gets older, those embarrassing moments; they don't matter. It's not about you and it sure isn't about the perception of others who know nothing of your life.

You'll have to suspend most of your long-held notions of traditional manhood. Find ways into his world that allow you to nurture and support him. Easy? Not at all, but well worth the effort. The modern philosopher and writer Robert Brault wrote, "You will find that if you really try to be a father, your child will meet you halfway." It may not be the usual, you take one step and he takes one. It might be, you take five and he takes one. Sometimes you take one forward and he takes one backward. Keep walking the journey with your son; you will get to a place of understanding, appreciation and life-affirming love. Just always be mindful that it's not about you.

As Julian moves into early adulthood, I look at him and realize that, in his own way, he is going to be one helluva man. You see, it's really about him.

THE MOST WONDERFUL TIME OF THE YEAR

"Mom, have you mailed my (Christmas) list yet?" Martina was standing in the kitchen facing me, with her back to Julian who had just posed that question. Yes, our nineteen-year-old son wanted to know if his Christmas wish list had been mailed to Santa. This caught us both a bit off-guard, so much so that we exchanged looks of mild shock and disbelief. Were we being *Punk'd?* Where was Ashton Kutcher? I was the first to respond.

"We didn't think you were finished putting it together." That was enough to give Julian pause.

"Uh-h maybe not, I have some other things I want."

Then Martina was able to chime in. "Good, when you're done, we'll get it off."

Julian's face lit up, he nearly levitated, and with a big smile, he said, "Great!" He clapped his hands, then bounded out of the room, obviously content that all communications would be relayed to the proper holiday authorities.

Later, I realized that exchange shouldn't have come as a complete surprise. A few days earlier, Julian, in the most casual manner, asked me when he would have the opportunity to speak with Santa. He was concerned that a recent meltdown of his might have been captured by the North Pole's monitoring apparatus. He wanted a chance to explain his actions and assure Santa that this would not happen again. I promised him I would arrange a phone call in the near future. My close friend Barry can sound quite jolly when he puts his mind to it. In fact, over the years, he has served as an understanding but firm Santa during annual conversations with Julian.

Julian and Santa have provided us with some memorable moments. When he was twelve, and still desiring an audience with the jolly one, we had to come up with the right solution. At this point he was tall for his age and Martina and I recognized that Julian standing in line at the mall, along with kids half his age, might make for some awkward and potentially uncomfortable moments, especially if someone said the wrong thing to Julian. I did some reconnaissance and found out that one of the shopping centers had really low traffic between two and four p.m. on weekdays.

So, on a day when Julian was released from school early, we met Martina at the shopping center. As we approached the center of the mall, there was Santa sitting on his chair, and only one other child and parent around. Perfect! We then introduced Julian to Santa, who was making eye contact with me to be sure this wasn't a joke. After greeting Julian and seeing the earnest look on his face, Santa knew what to do, and they had a very nice visit. Mission accomplished.

We finally convinced Julian, after one more year, that he could just as easily have a longer conversation with Santa over the telephone to make sure everything would be in order for that year. Barry, my "jolly" friend, began speaking with Julian and Jared when they were toddlers. It was neat to watch their faces as they spoke with Santa. Now Barry's role would simply be expanded and placed on an extended yearly run.

After Julian's query about his wish list, Martina and I wondered. Does he still believe? He can't possibly, can he? Kids at school, his brother, his friends; we knew he had heard the stories about how it was all a myth. Surely he knows it's Barry on the other end of the phone every December? He's just enjoying being part of our own little holiday theater, right? On some level we are certain Julian is well aware of the "realities" of Christmas. I recall numerous times, when he was between the ages of ten and twelve, when he would ask me whether or not Santa Claus was real. He was, constantly, hearing from other children, how it was all a big fantasy.

Martina and I always maintained to him that it was really about what he believed and the spirit of Christmas. If Julian were neurotypical, obviously, we would've had the conversation at some point to clear the air, as I did with Jared once he reached a certain age. However, with Julian, it is different. The holiday season means so much to him. In fact, with all due respect to Edward Pola and George Wyle, writers of the song, for Julian, "It's the Most Wonderful Time of the Year." Without a doubt, it occupies a very high position in Julian's world. I suspect Julian knows; he simply chooses to believe in the idea of Santa. Nothing wrong with that, it works for him and it works for us.

His excitement, in anticipation of Christmas, usually starts to build in late September. It generally begins with his informing us of the potential contents of his wish list. This always revolves around Disney animated movie DVDs, toy replicas of characters from said Disney movies and stuffed animals. That's pretty much what he asks for every year. It has been interesting and challenging for us to fulfill some of his requests. Try finding a toy version of Dr. Facilier from *The Princess and the Frog*. Martina usually does the sleuthing in this area. It took her nearly a full year of scouring toy stores and the Internet, but she was finally able to come across a complete set of characters from the movie, which included Dr. Facilier!

Another aspect of Julian's holiday buildup is the music. He loves listening to it and no time is too early. We've often heard Vanessa Williams' and Bobby Caldwell's version of "Baby, It's Cold Outside" coming from the CD player in his room, in July! This leads to a cute game of musical "cat and mouse" between Martina and Julian. She loves the holiday season as much as he does, but she needs everything in order. Therefore, for her, no Christmas music until the day after Thanksgiving.

In early November, Julian will begin to inquire about holiday music on the radio. Yes, several stations begin well before the Thanksgiving turkey has even been considered. I, having no such ordered thinking as Martina does, have no issue with Julian listening to Christmas music before it's appropriate. When he's in the car with me, then he quickly finds the holiday station. When Martina is in the car, he will inquire to make sure she hasn't changed her thinking on the matter. "Mom, do you think they're playing Christmas music yet?" he says, knowing full well that he's already been listening when she's not within earshot.

With a big smile, she offers, "I don't know, but it's not time yet." Yes, she is well aware that Julian has already begun getting his holiday music fix. And so it goes for most of November. Martina knows it's (the music) is there but doesn't want to know where it is, and Julian acts as though he's only occasionally heard a song or two, of course by accident.

Once Thanksgiving dinner is over, usually we are returning from celebrating with my family in South Carolina, Martina signals to Julian, who's bursting with enthusiasm, it's time and the two of them are off together, total immersion in the holiday spirit. I've never known two people who love that time of the year more, or get more enjoyment out of sharing that fondness for the season with each other. Our entire world—car, house, everything—

becomes swept up in the tide of the holiday season. Jared and I like it too, but we're amateur enthusiasts compared to Martina and Julian.

This all reaches a crescendo on Christmas Day when our house is filled with family, friends, a large dinner, considerable holiday cheer and one very happy Julian.

As for his earlier referenced Christmas list, he did eventually complete it and he watched me hand it to the mail carrier. As the mail truck pulled away, I watched my son, standing next to me, beaming and waving as the vehicle disappeared from view. There is nothing wrong with believing in something that brings one so special, such joy. I hope to see many more Christmases through the eyes and heart of Julian.

Julian walks on the beach in August 2008
Courtesy of Dwayne Ballen

THOUGHTS FROM FELLOW TRAVELERS

I asked a few people, all of whom I felt were representative of different viewpoints of Julian, to contribute their thoughts about him; anything they wanted to share was fine. I refer to them as fellow travelers on this Journey with Julian. Essays were written by Jared, Julian's younger brother; Will Arrington, a friend and member of Julian's social group; Tiffane Land, an autism advocate who has worked closely with Julian; and Ralph Tucker, one of Julian's teachers who has spent quite a bit of time with him. Finally, there is a letter from Martina to Julian.

I hope you enjoy the heartfelt and honest sentiments expressed by them over the next pages.

A little over fourteen years ago Will Arrington and Julian met; they would eventually become members of a quintet that comprised a social group for children with autism. In their own special way they are now good friends, which is quite a thing to be able to say about persons with autism.

MY FRIEND, JULIAN
BY WILL ARRINGTON

When I first met Julian, two things popped into my six-year-old head. The first, as was common for me in those days, was a physical observation. He had the most perfectly white teeth I had ever seen. He still does, so I have to give him major props for his dental care. But the second, and by far more important thought, was that I had just met a great new friend. Nearly fifteen years later, he still remains a great friend. Julian is one of the kindest people I've ever met, in addition to being one of the most inspiring.

Julian and I share a unique bond. It's not over-typical "boy" things like sports, girls, or action movies. Instead, we mostly talk about mythical creatures, a thing we both share a common interest in. These include creatures such as The Mothman, Bigfoot, or his personal favorite, the Salawa. It's always entertaining to talk about such things, and his near encyclopedic knowledge of such creatures always astounds me.

Through the years, Julian has also served as a role model. He's unfailingly polite, something I wholeheartedly admit I'm not. I recall one instance at a mutual friend's pool party. Julian heard me speaking to the friend's father and heard me call him "sir." I happened to look at him at that instant and saw that he was staring at me as if antlers had just sprouted out of my head. Curious, I asked him what had troubled him. He politely (and honestly) answered, "Nothing. It's just that's the first time I've seen you being polite."

While I took no offense to the statement, I did take it to heart. Now whenever faced with higher authority, I have found it effective to model him. This has served me very well, and I am indebted to Julian for this.

I also immensely admire his seemingly never-ending coolheadedness. In all the time I've known him, I have never once seen him angered by anybody or anything. It is always nice to know that he always keeps calm, and is usually always cheerful. I admire consistency in any person, and Julian's attitude toward people (one of happiness) is one of the primary reasons behind this.

His gifts as an artist never cease to amaze me. I can say without a shadow of a doubt, Julian is by far the most talented person I have ever personally met. I remember once he caught a glimpse of a friend's kitten running off to another room. He quickly asked for a pen and paper, and from that fleeting glimpse drew a near perfect portrait of that cat. He has, for years, told me of his love for Disney animation, and he is exceptionally gifted at drawing these as well. I have told him that he should pursue work at the company, and I do believe he will go places with his talents. I personally hope to one day have a drawing by him on my mantelpiece.

When I think of Julian, the fact he has autism doesn't pop in my mind. Instead, I think of what a wonderful human being he is. I do not believe Julian's autism will be a hindrance to his future. On the contrary, I think it forms an essential part of his personality. It makes him who he is: A wonderful human being, a cheerful optimist, a gifted artist, and just like he was that day fifteen years ago, a good friend. With perfect white teeth.

Ralph Tucker is one of Julian's teachers at the Lakeview Therapeutic Learning Center in Durham, NC. Mr. Tucker spends a great deal of time with Julian. When he and the other teachers first encountered Julian, it was right after his hospitalization. At that time Julian was a shell of his former self.

MY STUDENT, JULIAN
BY RALPH TUCKER

When I first met Julian, I did not know about any of his gifts, abilities, or of his bubbly personality. I had no point of reference as to who he had been or what he was capable of as a student, or as a person. Julian's mind and emotions had been stressed to a point of dysfunction and it was our challenge at the Therapeutic Learning Center to help him through this difficult time and to help him to recover, rediscover, and discover himself and his world. He barely spoke and would not write, type, or eat his lunch. In fact, watching Julian at that time, it would have been easy to assume that he did not hear or understand anything that was going on around him because he appeared to be so unexpressive and non-responsive. Sometimes students would talk around him as if he wasn't there, or as if he could not hear or understand what was being said.

One day while Julian was standing in line in the hallway with the other students, I noticed the slightest twitch in his cheek muscles that indicated to me that something had been said to irritate him. I continued to observe him and discovered that he listened intently to what students and staff said about him or other students and that his response was always reflected in almost invisible nonverbal cues. I am not sure if I had heard him speak at this point, but one day I asked him if he heard and understood some of the things that were being said about him or others. He nodded yes, and from that day I determined I would relate to the Julian who understood inside in order to help him to become more expressive and demonstrative of his skills and abilities. I found out that Julian, who was so mild mannered and well mannered, also had an angry side and a stubborn side. I had heard about his artistic abilities, but now he seemed paralyzed with a pencil in his hand and could not seem to write his own name or press one key on the computer keyboard. We searched for ways to motivate Julian to use even the slightest motor skills.

Day after day Julian would sit poised over his keyboard, over his lunch, or with his pencil in hand with no forward progression. Each day Julian looked forward to the time to go home. One day while sitting with him in the computer lab trying to get him to type one letter, I said to him that I would just sit there with him until he was able to type his name. When he seemed concerned that it might be time to go, I said that I was in no hurry and that I could sit there with him long after everyone had gone home. To my surprise he began to type.

As I continued to use that newfound leverage, I was surprised to find out that Julian could type much faster than I could have imagined. It also worked to get Julian to eat his lunch as well. I discovered that certain key words would trigger Julian to act when he seemed to get stuck and slip into lethargy. Movement words seemed to motivate him, so whenever I wanted to help him snap out of a stuck place, I would say, "Keep it moving, Julian," and he would get a look of determination on his face and stir himself into action.

As we began to find out what Julian was interested in and what would bring a smile to his face, we were able to relate to him through his interest and help him to come out of his cave of fear by getting him to talk about mythological figures, Disney characters, or anything about the Animal Kingdom. I overheard his mother say, in a meeting once, that Julian liked the Earth, Wind & Fire song, "Be Ever Wonderful," so sometimes I would play it in class when Julian seemed to be too consumed in thought to focus. Sometimes I think I also did it for myself, when I was feeling weary from the day, just to see Julian's excitement which seemed to change the mood of the entire classroom.

Watching Julian regain his confidence and self-esteem enabled us to see that Julian not only had interests and knowledge that amazed the staff and students, but that he had a gift to inspire enthusiasm in others. Julian's radiant smile, his exuberance, and excitement about life stimulated both students and staff. In staff meetings after a particularly difficult day, all one had to do to bring smiles and positive energy to the room was to speak of Julian. At his home school, the police officer who directs traffic talks about how it lifts his spirits each morning to see Julian get off of the van with such excitement and such a contagious smile.

It has been such a pleasure to know and work with Julian. Julian has sensitivity to the pain and discomfort of others that is not readily apparent in his communication with students and staff. Julian was not always comfortable asking a student if they were okay, if they looked sad or hurt, or if they were having an emotional episode or had to be redirected through staff intervention, but he often asked a teacher or staff person, "Is so-and-so okay?" If a student was absent for a period of time or had transitioned out of the school, Julian would often ask about their welfare. Julian is very concerned about his own future and what his life will become, but he also has a genuine interest in the well-being of others.

Julian's interest in, and knowledge of, Disney characters, mythological creatures or animals seems to provide a template for his understanding of the world. Sometimes in conversation with him, I get profound insights about life and I am able to share insights with him as we enter into his matrix of thought. Julian's love of animals, both real and mythological, is expressed with a concern for all sentient beings. As I noted earlier, sometimes Julian expresses his anger or annoyance, but one thing is clear to me: Julian has a heart of gold and as the police officer at his home school said, "A heart from God."

Jared is Julian's younger brother, by nearly twenty-four months. A neurotypical child, he has been through some rough patches with his brother as he has adjusted to life in the world of autism. What has endured is a strong brotherly bond of love and support.

MY BROTHER, JULIAN
BY JARED BALLEN

Julian Kendrick Ballen is my hero. He's been my best friend since I've been alive, a role model, and most importantly a loving brother. When I was younger, I thought it was so cool to have a big brother like Julian. He's been a joy to be around. His courage inspires me. Around the age of nine, I started noticing differences in my brother, compared to most children his age.

Julian wasn't as social; he kept more to himself, and would often pace back and forth when he got excited. Children would tease and make fun of my brother behind his back in elementary school. This used to upset me a great deal. At the time the teasing didn't upset me as much as the fact that I'd come to the realization that my brother was different, very different, from everyone else. All I wanted was for the behavior he exhibited to stop.

I specifically remember one evening when my father came into my room and explained to me that Julian had this neurological disorder called autism. At first I didn't really know how to process the information. If my memory serves me correctly, I think I asked my dad if it could be fixed. This term, autism, was in my head for a while, and I'd ask myself why it had to be my brother. It took a while, meaning a couple of years, to fully understand what my brother was dealing with in autism. Actually, we're quite fortunate that Julian's form of autism places him on the high-functioning end of the spectrum. Looking back on our lives together, up to this point, makes me realize how blessed, grateful, and privileged I am to have an awesome big brother like Julian.

Tiffane Land is a very passionate autism advocate. Julian first came into her orbit as a camper in a six-week summer program she runs for children with high-functioning autism. Over the years, she has been a champion for Julian and has come to know him quite well.

JULIAN, THE INSIGHTFUL ARTIST
BY TIFFANE LAND

I recently learned that when some spiders spin their web, they use a series of sticky and nonsticky silks within the complex pattern of the web. The nonsticky silks are the ones they use to walk on and the sticky silks are used to catch their prey. I do not know why I never questioned why spiders did not get stuck in their own webs, but it is now clear to me that the web must be entirely designed well before the first silk is emitted and that the web itself is far more impressive than I thought it was.

Julian's webs are his paintings. They are beautiful, vibrant, intricate masterpieces. I stand in awe as I watch him draw; knowing that, for him, he is simply transferring an exact design that he has already completed in his mind. He has a thousand pictures and facts of the same subject, from hundreds of perspectives and sources, concurrently present in his mind and he synthesizes all this into one, fairly exact depiction. One of his paintings is not a single image, it is a summary; and, therefore, far more impressive.

Like his paintings, Julian is intricate…and impressive. He is passionate, determined, and focused. He is quiet, yet thoughtful. He is polite, respectful, and eager. He can be pensive, yet his smile and laughter will exude such purity and pleasure. He is creative with a capacious mind and a gentle sense of humor. He is often in need of reassurance, yet he will have moments of such boldness and strength. He is truehearted, innocent, and optimistic. His autism is only the filter through which all this is seen. He is inspiring.

I first met Julian in the fall of 2008. Becoming part of Julian's journey meant that he instantly became part of mine. There are numerous moments that I can recall; each one a time when I recognized that I was perhaps leaving it with more gained than given. The resounding theme that has developed from this "apprenticeship" under Julian is that, in general, the same aspirations and life-long objectives lie within us all. Having autism does not change this. Finding a way to get there is part of everyone's journey and we all need support, different kinds of support, to get there. Having autism does not change this either.

Martina was in love the moment she gave birth to Julian. His autism forced her into a world she never anticipated. In an effort to know all she could to enable our son to have the best life possible, she has thrust herself into this with gusto. She recently stepped down as board chair for the Autism Society of North Carolina. She is constantly on the lookout for programs and events to keep Julian engaged with the world. She is a fiercely committed mother.

A LETTER TO MY SON
BY MARTINA BALLEN

Dear Julian,

I have loved you and believed in you from the moment you entered this world. What a joy to have a new baby boy named Julian Kendrick (my maiden name) Ballen. You have been a constant companion during shopping forays with Mom and me, along with patiently attending countless sporting events with Dad, Jared and me, hosted by Carolina Athletics (even though you aren't a sports fan). Your artistic ability was uncovered during a visit at (your late) Grandma Kendrick's church, where she gave you pen and paper to keep you occupied during the sermon. You haven't stopped drawing since that time!!!

I often smile when I think of the sheer joy you have when you visit Disney World or when you watch your favorite Disney movie. I love the fact that you enjoy R&B music as much as I do and we sometimes get lost in rhythmic movements while listening to Al Green or Jill Scott. I love the way your face lights up when you discover that you are having your favorite Chinese dish or Gramma

Ballen's macaroni and cheese. I can count on you to look after our dog, Tango. I am amazed at how you can draw Mickey Mouse, Simba from *The Lion King*, or any other Disney character or exotic animal with such swiftness and accuracy. We are joined in our eternal love of all things Christmas!

I hurt when you hurt. I am sad when you are sad. It pains me when I can't comfort you or help you work through a difficult time. I know that you struggle with finding ways to cope with anxiety, sadness or awkward social situations. As a mom, I want to make it better, but I know that I can't always find a solution. I will always be here for you, though, to help you navigate difficult times by offering comfort and support when there seems to be no other answer.

You are my hero. I have seen you go through a very dark period in your young life, only to have the will and desire to get to a better place. I know that you struggle with clearly seeing what your future will be, but none of us knows what the future holds. I am resolute in my belief that you can and will have a life full of love and promise, because Julian, I have loved you and believed in you from the moment you entered this world.

Love 4ever,
Mom

THE JOURNEY CONTINUES

As I conclude the writing of this book, Julian is nineteen years of age and a senior in high school. He is part of a rapidly growing community of young adults with autism. In the United States 50,000 turn eighteen every year. I'm hopeful that we, as a society, will begin to substantively address how to help make a place for them in our world. I don't mean simply to take care of them, but to help them reach their goals and find their respective places in life.

We should recognize the deep reservoir of talent and resources they possess. It is incumbent upon all of us to find ways to access those attributes. If for no other reason, think in selfish terms. Wouldn't you want all talented "hands on deck" to help address the issues facing this world? Why ignore a gifted segment of the population because they don't fit under the rubric of neurotypical?

I'm especially heartened by the efforts of a number of social entrepreneurs, researchers, business and civic leaders. Danish innovator Thorkil Sonne started a company, Specialisterne, which employs people with autism. He realized that certain jobs which require intense focus to detail, such as data entry and software testing, are in quite a few cases, perfectly suited for someone with autism. Recognized by the World Economic Forum for his work, Mr. Sonne, who has a son with autism, is bringing his idea to the U.S.

All of us connected to the world of autism, especially those who are in the role of caregivers, must always be mindful that just because the person, in our life, with autism is doing something unconventional, it doesn't mean that it is wrong. Always look at that person for who they are, their gifts. How can those be utilized to help them get the most out of life and, quite possibly, be an asset to greater society. I do feel that all the "Julians" in this world have been placed here to teach us something about ourselves and what truly matters. We must do more than merely look at them; we must use insight, understanding and a belief in the possibility of what can be.

In his seminal work "Invisible Man," Ralph Ellison's nameless protagonist informs the reader that he is invisible. It's not because he is some indiscernible apparition but, as he profoundly puts it, "I am invisible, understand, simply because people refuse to see me." We can never let that be the case with persons with autism, or any group that doesn't fit traditional cultural profiles. They all have something to offer; we just need to have sight.

Aside from professing his desire to work in animation for Disney, Julian has demonstrated a strong interest in what the future holds for him. We have regular discussions about this subject. The combination of mental illness and autism would've knocked someone of lesser mettle down and out. That's not Julian; he has displayed courage and resilience time and again.

He would like to be married one day, or at least the concept seems to appeal to him. He's asked me what he should name his children. As I noted earlier in this book, those conversations are especially hard. While I want so much for it to happen for him, I understand the realities of his life as a person with autism. That doesn't mean I don't believe and hope that he can experience those aspects of life. I simply know Julian and what it would require of anyone to build that sort of a relationship with him. It would be one of the greatest days of my life to stand at his wedding or to simply know that he is in a committed and loving partnership with someone. Martina and I will always hold out hope for the possibility of "what can be."

I do feel that he has something to contribute to this world. His creativity and imagination are immense and seem boundless. In addition he is very caring and considerate. Qualities that I know will serve him well in the years ahead.

He and I have embarked on our own project together, an animated story about a family of wolves. I'm not certain where the journey will take us from here. I only know that it continues, with Julian showing the way.

A JULIAN BALLEN GALLERY

On the following pages are some of Julian's many drawings of members of the animal kingdom.

Elephant, 2007
Courtesy of Julian Ballen

Giraffe, 2009
Courtesy of Julian Ballen

Impalas in South Africa, 2009
Courtesy of Julian Ballen

Red Fox, 2012
Courtesy of Julian Ballen

Wildebeest, 2007
Courtesy of Julian Ballen

Malaysian Tarsier, 2006
Courtesy of Julian Ballen

Tiger, 2008
Courtesy of Julian Ballen

Julian at a family picnic in 2011
Courtesy of Dwayne Ballen

ACKNOWLEDGMENTS

I am forever indebted to the myriad people without whom this book could not have been written. First, and foremost, my son Julian who has taught me more than I thought any child could teach a parent. He has allowed me to share intimate details of our life in the hope that it will help other families living with autism realize they are not alone and to raise awareness about the world of autism. Julian is a constant source of inspiration and will forever be my hero.

My partner in this experience is my amazing wife, Martina. Without her unconditional support and love, I would never have reached the level of comfort and, hopefully, understanding required to write this book. When I needed encouragement, she encouraged. When I needed prodding, she prodded and quite well I might add. This sojourn through the world of autism has been no easy trip for our younger son, Jared. He has found a way to carve out a very special relationship with his big brother. Watching his growth and acceptance of Julian's autism fills me with pride. Gayle Stephens served as the boys' nanny during their formative years. She was considerate, nurturing and loving. Especially in her handling and caring for Julian. We can never repay what she gave to our sons.

Essential to Julian's success has been the care and guidance of what amounts to a small army of determined teachers, advocates and health professionals. Some of whom are Karen Rodenhizer, Willa Sample, Ralph Tucker, Tiffane Land, Wanda Brown, Evan Kirasawa, Kathleen Wright, Ms. Duncan at Hope Valley Elementary, Dr. Warnele Carmon, Jess Reiniger, Jack Allen, Willis Foster, Francis Beamon, the entire staff of the Lakeview Therapeutic Learning Center, Scott Badesch and his staff at the Autism Society of America, Linda Newmark and Dr. Lin Sikich. These are only a few of the persons who have used their professional expertise in concert with a genuine feeling for Julian to aid him in his journey.

A special thank you is owed to Linda Varblow. An autism learning specialist who, in 2001, opened her home to Julian and four other children (including her son Joey) with high-functioning autism and started what, today, is known as "The Social Group." The weekly gathering of this group has continued for over ten years. Thanks to her they are not only confident and comfortable with their autism but, maybe most important, they have formed bonds of friendship which, I suspect, will last for life. We are forever indebted to Ms. Varblow and the entire social group family.

Tracey Sheriff, David Laxton and the entire staff and board of the Autism Society of North Carolina have provided support and enlightenment. Their Camp Royall retreat has become one of Julian's favorite places to spend time.

Will Arrington, Ralph Tucker and Tiffane Land were all very gracious with their time and consideration as they committed to write essays about their respective views of Julian. They have helped to enrich this book.

The love of family and friends has made the journey a celebration of Julian and has eased the pain during difficult times. I can't imagine traveling this road without the (collective) outreached arms and shoulders of support provided by the late

Ruth Kendrick (Grandma Kendrick to Julian); my mom, Doris Ballen (Gramma Ballen); Uncle Harold & Aunt Pearl; my siblings, Rod, Kolton, Iris and Mike and their families; Martina's brother and sister, Martin Kendrick and Pam McDonald and their families; the numerous relatives and friends who always wanted to know how Julian was doing, Barry Saunders who has a pair of the strongest shoulders anyone could lean on, Reggie & Ranota Hall (Uncle Reggie & Aunt Ranota to Julian), Julian's godmother, (Aunt) Devetta Holman, Rohena Miller, my dear friend and CEO of Niche Marketing, who came up with the title and encouraged me to write this book and the blog, Cricket Lane & Jeff Eisen, Gil Fitts, Annette Gibbs, Stephanie Thompson-Harris (Aunt Stephanie), Scott Long, Deborah Thomas, Patti & Holden Thorp, Beth Miller, Rick & Valerie Steinbacher, Larry Gallo, Sam Paul and Martina's wonderful colleagues at UNC. All of these people have added value to Julian's life.

When Julian began taking his solo walks throughout our neighborhood, in search of creatures, I always knew that extra eyes were watching, from a distance, to make sure he was okay. To Mike, Rahul, Mannar and all our neighbors, thanks for helping to provide us with an extra sense of comfort whenever Julian decided to go on expedition.

When I asked my friend, Branford Marsalis, the great jazz musician, to write the foreword, I was well aware of how hectic his touring schedule gets, once I texted him about having dinner and his response was sure, if I could make it to Copenhagen by six. I knew from previous conversations that he really understood, because of his own family experience, what it meant to be in the autism community, so I wanted his input. A deep thanks to him for taking time to share his thoughts and words.

Finally I want to thank my editor, Charmaine Parker of Strebor Books/Simon & Schuster. Without her patience and belief in my abilities, this book might still just be an idea in my head.

Thank you all for booking passage with Julian and our family on this journey.